THE PSYCHOLOGY OF THE TEENAGE BRAIN

Why do teenagers stay up late and struggle to get up in the morning? Do teenagers really take more risks? What is happening with teenagers' hormones?

The Psychology of the Teenage Brain offers all those involved in teenagers' lives insight into what's happening in their brains and how understanding them can improve relationships and communication at this crucial stage. It explains key topics, including the way the brain changes during adolescence, the role of hormones, and what we really know about risk and resilience, sleep and peer pressure. It challenges the stereotype of the "snowflake generation" and explores young people's mental health.

Written for all parents and caregivers, this book will help with the challenges of having a teenager in the home. It also offers crucial understanding for all students and practising professionals in the fields of social work, counselling, health and education who work with teenagers.

John Coleman trained as a clinical psychologist and was formerly a senior research fellow at the University of Oxford. He is the founder of a research centre studying adolescents and their families, and during his career he has also run a special school for troubled teenagers and worked as a policy advisor for the government. He was awarded an OBE for services to young people in the Queen's Birthday Honours in 2001.

THE PSYCHOLOGY OF EVERYTHING

People are fascinated by psychology, and what makes humans tick. Why do we think and behave the way we do? We've all met armchair psychologists claiming to have the answers, and people that ask if psychologists can tell what they're thinking. The Psychology of Everything is a series of books which debunk the popular myths and pseudo-science surrounding some of life's biggest questions.

The series explores the hidden psychological factors that drive us, from our subconscious desires and aversions, to our natural social instincts. Absorbing, informative, and always intriguing, each book is written by an expert in the field, examining how research-based knowledge compares with popular wisdom, and showing how psychology can truly enrich our understanding of modern life.

Applying a psychological lens to an array of topics and contemporary concerns – from sex, to fashion, to conspiracy theories – The Psychology of Everything will make you look at everything in a new way.

Titles in the series:

The Psychology of Grief
by Richard Gross

The Psychology of Sex
by Meg-John Barker

The Psychology of Dieting
by Jane Ogden

The Psychology of Performance
by Stewart T. Cotterill

The Psychology of Trust
by Ken J. Rotenberg

The Psychology of Working Life
by Toon W. Taris

The Psychology of Conspiracy Theories
by Jan-Willem van Prooijen

The Psychology of Addiction
by Jenny Svanberg

The Psychology of Fashion
by Carolyn Mair

The Psychology of Gardening
by Harriet Gross

The Psychology of Gender
by Gary Wood

The Psychology of Climate
Change
by Geoffrey Beattie and Laura McGuire

The Psychology of Vampires
by David Cohen

The Psychology of Chess
by Fernand Gobet

The Psychology of Music
by Susan Hallam

The Psychology of Weather
by Trevor Harley

The Psychology of Driving
by Graham J. Hole

The Psychology of
Retirement
by Doreen Rosenthal and Susan M. Moore

The Psychology of School
Bullying
by Peter Smith

The Psychology of Celebrity
by Gayle Stever

The Psychology of Dog
Ownership
by Craig Roberts and Theresa Barlow

The Psychology of Social Media
by Ciarán Mc Mahon

The Psychology of Happiness
by Peter Warr

The Psychology of Politics
by Barry Richards

The Psychology of the
Paranormal
by David Groome

The Psychology of Prejudice
by Richard Gross

The Psychology of Intelligence
by Sonja Falck

The Psychology of Terrorism
by Neil Shortland

The Psychology of Dreaming
by Josie Malinowski

The Psychology of Exercise
by Josephine Perry

The Psychology of Video Games
by Celia Hodent

The Psychology of Religion
by Vassilis Saroglou

The Psychology of Belonging
by Kelly-Ann Allen

The Psychology of Art
by George Mather

The Psychology of Wellness
by Gary W. Wood

The Psychology of Comedy
by G Neil Martin

The Psychology of Democracy
by Darren G. Lilleker and Billur Aslan Ozgul

The Psychology of Counselling
by Marie Percival

The Psychology of Travel
by Andrew Stevenson

The Psychology of Attachment
by Robbie Duschinsky, Pehr Granqvist and Tommie Forslund

The Psychology of Running
by Noel Brick and Stuart Holliday

For more information about this series, please visit:
www.routledgetextbooks.com/textbooks/thepsychologyofeverything/

THE PSYCHOLOGY OF
THE TEENAGE BRAIN

JOHN COLEMAN

LONDON AND NEW YORK

Cover image: © Getty Images

First published 2024
by Routledge
4 Park Square, Milton Park, Abingdon, Oxon OX14 4RN

and by Routledge
605 Third Avenue, New York, NY 10158

Routledge is an imprint of the Taylor & Francis Group, an informa business

© 2024 John Coleman

British Library Cataloguing-in-Publication Data
A catalogue record for this book is available from the British Library

ISBN: 978-1-032-36393-6 (hbk)
ISBN: 978-1-032-36395-0 (pbk)
ISBN: 978-1-003-33172-8 (ebk)

DOI: 10.4324/9781003331728

Typeset in Joanna
by Apex CoVantage, LLC

CONTENTS

Acknowledgements   ix
List of images   xi

1   Introduction to the teenage brain   1

2   Introduction to teenage development   13

3   Raging hormones   22

4   Learning, learning, learning   35

5   The social brain   50

6   Wide awake at midnight   63

7   Is this the "snowflake generation"?   75

8   The teenage brain for key adults   90

References   103

ACKNOWLEDGEMENTS

This book would not have been possible without the assistance and support of numerous people. First and foremost, I should acknowledge David Silverman and Joella Scott, whose enthusiasm got the "My Teen Brain" project in Hertfordshire underway. My colleagues at Family Links, especially Sarah Darton, Kathy Peto and Rowen Smith, have contributed their skills as trainers and enabled the project to be such a success. A number of organizations have played their part, including Bounce Forward, the Charlie Waller Trust, Parenting Northern Ireland and the Association for Young People's Health. I would like to thank all those amazing teachers whose enthusiasm for the project encouraged me and gave me access to schools. Lastly, this work could not have happened without the students who generously gave their time helping me to explore and understand what is happening in their brains during the teenage years.

IMAGES

1.1 The sites of the brain (Taken from list of illustrations
Art No. 3)   5

1.2 The synapse (Taken from list of illustrations Art No. 5)   6

3.1 The nucleus accumbens (Taken from list of illustrations
Art No. 23)   27

4.1 New receptors are added to synapses during learning
(Taken from list of illustrations Art No. 18)   37

4.2 Inhibition and the on/off mechanism (Taken from
list of illustrations Art No. 7)   38

4.3 Two graphs showing changes in white and grey matter
(Taken from list of illustrations Art No. 20).   39

1

INTRODUCTION TO THE TEENAGE BRAIN

INTRODUCTION

This book is about the teenage years. However, I am not approaching it in the usual way. I am going to write about all the important things – about friends and peer groups, about parenting, about young people having a good time, about teens not being able to get to sleep, about mental health, and so on. But I am going to write about these topics from the perspective of brain development.

You may, at first, find this strange. You may think this is too scientific for you. You may want to learn how to communicate better with your teenager. You may be looking for tips about how to avoid conflict. You may even be wringing your hands about their social media use. Why do you need to know about the brain?

In this book, I will show you that understanding the brain will give you a completely different picture of the teenage years. For centuries, teenagers have puzzled, confused and infuriated adults. Why is it that young people have to argue about everything that adults say? Why are they so contradictory – happy one moment and cast into despair the next? How is it that a normal chatty child has turned into a bad-tempered recluse?

I will argue that the clue is in the brain. Once parents, teachers and others learn what is happening in the teenage brain, they can see that the confusing behaviour makes sense. For the last few years, I have

DOI: 10.4324/9781003331728-1

been running groups for parents in which I outline the main facts about brain development. The result?

Parents talk about a "light-bulb moment". They report a complete change of attitude to their son or daughter. "Wow! I really didn't know all this," said one parent to me. "I will be so much more sympathetic now." Another said: "This will change the way I relate to my 15-year-old." "Thank you, thank you," said another. "If only we had understood this earlier so many problems might have been avoided."

I believe that this knowledge really does have the potential to change family relationships. Of course, there are other factors at play. I will discuss these at various points during the book. One big factor is the social circumstances that affect all teenagers. At what point are they grown up? When can they take decisions for themselves? What rights do parents have over health and educational choices? These questions highlight the fact that the teenage years are a transition from child to adult. And transitions can be uncomfortable. There will be more about transitions in Chapter 2.

I will show that it will be much easier to deal with the questions thrown up by the process of transition if we take into account the impact of the changes in the brain. I very much hope that you will find this information helpful in your relationships with the teenagers in your life.

INTRODUCTION TO THE BRAIN

The brain is a mystery. It is also a thing of wonder. The human brain is the most complex entity in nature. It is quite small – you can hold it in your hands. It is an organ, but it acts as a machine, a controller, a manifestation of human evolution, and it is the single most determining feature of each and every one of us.

It is a mystery because there is still so much we do not know about the brain. While neuroscience has made huge strides in the last 20 years, we are still at the very beginning of the search for a full understanding of the brain. Some writers call the brain "the inner cosmos". This is because it has a capacity that is so vast and because it is mostly as yet unexplored.

I call it a thing of wonder because the feats the brain performs are remarkable. Our brains manage our emotions, determine our actions, store our memories, create our dreams, help us deal with threats, and basically keep us alive by regulating temperature, blood levels, energy and the sleep/wake cycle.

In this chapter, I will explain, as clearly as I can, the basic processes that take place when we think, feel, relate and respond to our environment. However, this book is about the teenage brain, so I also want to outline the key changes that occur during the adolescent years. Until quite recently, it was believed that the brain stopped developing at the end of childhood. We knew very little about what happens to the brain after puberty.

Since the advent of scanning, the picture has changed completely. We now know that the brain undergoes major changes during the teenage years. These changes have profound implications for the way teenagers behave and the way they deal with the challenges of this stage of life.

A SHORT DESCRIPTION OF THE HUMAN BRAIN

The brain contains billions of cells. You will have heard people talk about "little grey cells". Your brain contains in the region of 80 billion "little grey cells". These cells are known as neurons. This is an unimaginable number. In fact, the joke is that the human brain cannot comprehend that number of neurons! This is a number that is nearly ten times more than the entire global population.

All these billions of neurons are connected to other neurons in patterns and networks. We still know little about how these neurons combine together. It is hard to understand how the billions and billions of neurons can work together without getting into a tangle in the small space that is the human brain.

All our bodily systems are powered by the oxygen in our bloodstream, and the brain is no exception. The brain also uses electrical and chemical processes to send messages along the pathways that connect the neurons together. These pathways are the nerve fibres that stretch across and around the brain. Each neuron has a number of nerve fibres reaching out to other neurons in the system. Messages or impulses are carried around the brain along these nerve fibres.

One remarkable feature of the brain is that there is a tiny gap in the nerve fibre or branch that reaches out from every neuron. This gap is called a **synapse**, and it means that the message or impulse has to jump over the gap to reach the next neuron. This is an important part of the picture, and I will say more about the synapse in a minute.

In order to understand the brain, we need to picture the different roles that various parts of it perform. As I said, the brain is immensely complex, so I will just concentrate on the most important sites. This will help you, the reader, to get a sense of the key elements of the structure of the brain. The first part I want to mention is known as the **prefrontal cortex**. This site is associated with thinking, reasoning and problem-solving. Some people like to call it the "command and control" centre. It is located at the front of the brain and can be considered as the rational, sensible part of the brain which helps us think about the consequences of our actions.

The second site to mention is the **amygdala**. This is located deep in the middle of the brain and is the part that processes and manages our emotions. The amygdala is that feature of the brain that determines our feelings, but it is also the site that is most affected by stress and difficult experiences. The third part of the brain to mention is the **hippocampus**. This is where memory is processed and stored for a short time until it is passed on to long-term memory.

THE SYNAPSE

I have already mentioned the synapse. This tiny gap plays an important part in the story of the brain. Within this gap are what are known as neurotransmitters. They are essentially chemical messengers, as they help or hinder the sending of impulses along the nerve fibres. Another way to think about the synapse is to think of it as an on/off mechanism. The chemical messengers within the synapse are a bit like traffic lights, showing green to indicate go, or showing red to indicate stop.

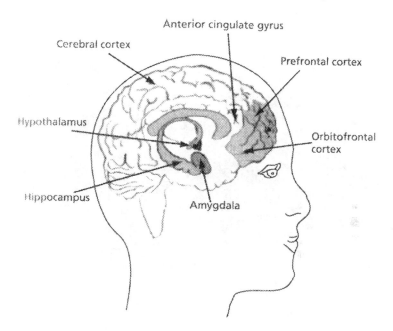

Figure 1.1 The sites of the brain

Some people liken this system to an air-traffic control set-up. I prefer to think about it as a railway network. If there was no signalling system, the trains would bump into each other and the system would come to a standstill. Imagine the multitude of neurons and networks all sending trillions of messages all the time in your brain. Without some form of signalling, there would be chaos!

Take a moment to think about yourself while you are reading this. You are bombarded by an enormous number of stimuli. You could concentrate on the noises outside the room, the ache in one of your muscles, the memories you have about what happened at breakfast, the worries you have about the work you are meant to be doing, and so on. It is easy for us to become overwhelmed by the sheer volume of possible stimuli. We would not be able to concentrate or pay attention if we did not have a system for blocking out the distractions.

This is especially important for young people in the classroom. The on/off mechanism is essential if they are to concentrate. And yet,

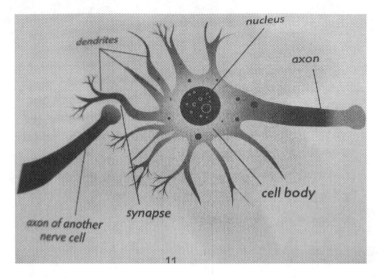

Figure 1.2 The synapse

there are those who find this difficult. For them, the mechanism is not working as well as it should. We will return to this topic later in the book.

SCANNING

The last 20 years have seen a gigantic leap forward in our understanding of the human brain. This is because of the development of the technology of scanning. It is now possible to take pictures of the brain as it functions, without any distress or discomfort. In previous years, this would have been considered impossible. The technology is known as brain imaging, or, to be technical, magnetic resonance imaging (MRI). What does this mean? This technology allows us to see how much oxygen is going to different parts of the brain at any one time. This is a huge advance, as it enables us to see which parts of the brain are active under different conditions. However, scanning can only tell us so much. It does not tell us what a person is thinking. There is also a limit to what we can tell about how the different networks combine and work together.

It is worth noting that, even in the last decade or so, there have been huge advances in the technology of scanning. In the early days, the process would have involved the individual lying on a bed and going into a tunnel. This would have been quite noisy and would have required the person to lie still for about 30 to 40 minutes. As a result, you could not use the technology in the classroom or when the person was moving around. Recently, the technology has advanced, so that mobile scanners are now available. This means that we can learn more about brain activity in a wider range of circumstances, and with a wider range of individuals.

THE CHANGING TEENAGE BRAIN

It is now time to turn to the changes that take place during the teenage years. The adolescent period can be a confusing and contradictory time of life. The young person is growing and changing. While the individual is still a child, he or she is also becoming an adult. This period is a major transition. I like to say that inside every teenager is BOTH a child and an adult. This contradiction means that things are often topsy-turvy. The young person can be happy and sad, grown up and needy, all at the same time. Most importantly for us, this contradiction is reflected in the brain.

On the one hand, the brain is maturing, allowing the young person to develop new skills and capabilities. On the other hand, the brain is also undergoing a major re-organization, leading to times of confusion and uncertainty. I will deal with the positives first.

All parts of the brain will mature during the years from puberty onwards. This maturation leads to increased skills and capacities in all areas, whether these be physical abilities, sexual maturation or cognitive functions. As you may imagine, one of the key areas here is the prefrontal cortex. It is this part of the brain which is most active during the learning process. Maturation here allows for better memory, improved vocabulary and the development of scientific reasoning. Better communication skills will also be developing. Adults sometimes find this hard to comprehend, but watching young people with their friends makes this plain to see.

In addition to the maturation of the brain, other things are happening, too. During the period around puberty, there is an overproduction of neurons and connections. At first sight, this may seem a strange thing to happen. In fact, this has happened earlier in childhood as well. What happens then is known as **pruning**. More neurons than can be accommodated have been produced, and as a result the brain allows the unwanted neurons and connections to die away. In the long run, this leads to a positive outcome. We sometimes say it leads to a "meaner, leaner machine"!

It is inevitable that this process leads to a significant restructuring and re-organization of the brain. Some scientists reckon that, on average, the brain loses 17% of the grey matter during the teenage years. Imagine what you would think if I were to tell you that you were going to lose so much of your brain in the next few years! It is a daunting thought. And it is no wonder that the process leads to times of confusion and uncertainty. As I have said, the outcome is positive. It allows the brain to function more efficiently. However, there is some cost in the process of actually getting there.

One other fact should be considered here. This has to do with the role of hormones. I am going to devote a whole chapter to hormones (Chapter 3). For the present, however, I do need to outline something of the way that hormones play a part in the changing brain. This is a period when there is an upset in the hormone balance. Readers will know that the teenage years are sometimes described as a time of "raging hormones". We can see this in common behaviours such as mood swings and the flip-flop of emotions.

One of the things we have learnt as a result of research on the teenage brain is that there is a marked level of variation in the hormone balance in this age group. All of us have some daily variation in the balance of hormones in our brains. The variation for teenagers, however, is much greater than for other age groups. Thus, the level of any of the key hormones may be going up or down to a significant extent in any one 24-hour period. It is not surprising, then, that this affects behaviour and means that emotion regulation is that much harder for young people.

HOW DOES THE BRAIN MATURE?

I have talked about maturation, but what does this actually mean? How does the brain mature? There are a number of processes that contribute to this. In the first place, I need to mention myelin. This is an extremely important substance that surrounds, encases and protects the nerve fibres. It also ensures that they remain separate from each other. If you remember how many neurons there are, and thus how many nerve fibres, you can see that it is essential to have a means of preventing the billions of fibres from getting tangled up.

As for maturation, during the teenage years, the myelin gets thicker. Clearly, this is at an infinitesimal level, but nonetheless the myelin gets thicker. This enables impulses to travel round the brain faster and more efficiently. This process takes some years, but it contributes significantly to a more mature and effective brain.

The second element that contributes to maturation has to do with the way both halves of the brain work together. One thing I haven't mentioned before is that the brain is in two halves. Why the human brain has two halves is a mystery, but there it is. Sometimes known as hemispheres, these two halves have to work together and in order for this to happen, there is a bridge between the two halves which is how they are connected.

During the teenage years, this bridge undergoes a major change. The connections between the two halves gradually increase, so that more information can be passed across. This also means that the individual can make use of greater brain capacity. This feature of the brain is known as connectivity. In essence, the more connectivity there is, the better the person's thinking abilities. If we want to understand intelligence, then we need to look at connectivity. In earlier times, it was believed that the size of a person's brain was a clue to their intelligence. We now know that this belief is false. Intelligence is not related to size, but to the connectivity between the two halves of the brain.

I should make one last point about maturation. During the teenage years, maturation does not occur equally across different parts of the brain. In fact, the brain matures from back to front. This is important because it means that the prefrontal cortex, the site of thinking and reasoning, is maturing at a slower rate than other sites in the brain. Of course, the prefrontal cortex is maturing, but it is just maturing more slowly than other parts of the brain.

When the first research studies started appearing in the early 2000s, these findings led scientists to argue that they had found the reason why some teenagers were likely to take risks. We have now learnt that this is much too simple an explanation. I will be talking a lot more about risk and risk-taking in Chapter 3.

THE BRAIN AND THE ENVIRONMENT

What determines the way the brain develops? This is a perennial question. Is it down to the person's genes? Is the structure of the brain set from the very early years? How does the environment make a difference to the way the brain develops in the teenage years? Do early experiences have later consequences?

I consider this to be a central question, but it is not an easy one to answer. The first important thing to note is that the brain and the environment interact. Each has an influence on the other. The environment has an effect on brain development, but the capacity of the brain will influence the way the individual responds to circumstances. As one example of this, it is probable that enriching environments lead to healthier brain development. On the other hand, environments that are restricted in one way or another are likely to hinder brain development.

This was a question that scientists were asking in the 1960s, when I was at university. We were taught about studies that placed rats in two different environments. One was full of toys and stimulating experiences, while the other environment was bare and spartan. The results were clear. The rats brought up in the stimulating environment were quicker learners and performed better at solving puzzles and finding their way around mazes.

In recent times, the experiences of Romanian orphans have given us a real-life opportunity to study this question. Readers may remember that, during the Ceausescu era in Romania, orphans were placed in extremely restricted environments, left in their cots with very little human contact. Many in the West offered to adopt these orphans, and this led to a number of natural experiments.

In the UK, the Institute of Psychiatry in London, led by Professor Michael Rutter, studied these orphans as they grew up, went to school and developed into teenagers. The results are fascinating. I will just mention two main findings. Firstly, the earlier the orphans were adopted, the easier it was to overcome the early deprivation. Those adopted before the age of one did better than those adopted between two and three years of age. This makes sense, as those adopted at a young age had a shorter experience of deprivation, and presumably there was less damage to the developing brain.

Those adopted later, however, also showed the capacity to recover. This group were able to make good relationships with their adoptive parents and were able to perform adequately at school. In spite of this, there remained some challenges for those adopted after the age of one. Once they got to secondary school, they struggled with friendships and showed other signs of finding it hard to adapt to changing circumstances such as the move to a new school.

One other strand of work casts some light on this question. In recent years, a number of studies have looked at teenage brain development in those who had been the subject to what are known as ACEs (adverse childhood experiences). Under this heading are usually included abuse, bereavement, rejection and other types of trauma. Results of these studies do show that, in some young people, early experiences lead to altered brain function. However, studies also show that the brain has the capacity to recover. Where the individual receives strong support and care, it would appear that earlier disadvantages can be overcome.

From all this, we can conclude that the environment really does make a difference. One key aspect of the environment for young people is, of course, the adults who surround them. This is an important message. Adults have a key role to play. All the research shows that outcomes for young people are very much affected by the support and engagement that is available from the adult world. This applies whether you are a parent, carer, teacher or other practitioner. The brain and the environment interact, and we will explore the ways in which this works over the course of this book.

CONCLUSION

I started this chapter by indicating that I will approach the teenage years from the perspective of the changing brain. I said that this might be a surprise to readers. However, I believe that knowing what happens in the brain leads to a complete change in the way we understand teenagers. In this chapter, I have covered the main changes that occur during the adolescent period. I have discussed scanning and outlined what it means to say the brain is maturing. I have discussed the relation between the brain and the environment, and showed that each influences the other. One young man said to me: "So, my brain is changing. Nothing much I can do about it then?" I was able to reassure him. The brain is not fixed. The environment makes a difference. There is a lot we can do to assist healthy brain development. I hope this book will lead to a better understanding of this remarkable organ in our heads.

FURTHER READING

Blakemore, S-J (2019) "*Inventing ourselves: the secret life of the teenage brain*". Transworld Publishers/Penguin. London.

Coleman, J (2021) "*The teacher and the teenage brain*". Routledge. Abingdon, Oxon.

Crone, E (2017) "*The adolescent brain: changes in learning, decision-making and social relations*". Psychology Press/Routledge. Abingdon, Oxon.

Eagleman, D (2015) "*The brain: the story of you*". Canongate. Edinburgh.

Scott, S (2022) "*The brain: 10 things you should know*". Orion Publishing. London.

2

INTRODUCTION TO TEENAGE DEVELOPMENT

INTRODUCTION

In the first chapter, I outlined the key facts about brain development. This will help readers grasp the scale of the changes that are taking place at this stage of life. I will now turn to other aspects of teenage development. This will put the changes to the brain in a more familiar context.

One of the questions I am frequently asked is, when do the teenage years start and when do they end? This is not an easy question to answer, since there are such large individual differences. As we shall see when we come to discuss puberty in Chapter 3, this key event can occur at 9 or 10, but it can also occur at 13 or 14. As a result, it is not easy to pinpoint the exact time when adolescence begins.

It is even more complex at the other end of the age range. As social changes have impacted on those aged 18 and over, it becomes harder to leave adolescence behind and achieve full adult status. More individuals remain living in the family home today than ever before. This is partly to do with housing, but it also has to do with the economic circumstances of young adults. In addition, more find their entry into the world of employment takes longer than in previous generations.

One of the most interesting findings from the research that I outlined in Chapter 1 is that some of the changes in the brain continue

DOI: 10.4324/9781003331728-2

into the early 20s. This fact underlines the point that development continues long after the word "teenager" can apply. In this book, I will be concentrating mainly on those in the secondary age range, that is, from 11 to 18. Nonetheless, it is worth keeping in mind that the age group between 18 and 24, most often known as young adults, will experience continuing changes. Simply because young people have left school does not mean that development has ceased.

TRANSITION

In the first chapter, I outlined what is clearly a major transition – from an immature brain to a rapidly maturing one. However, there are other aspects of transition that may be helpful to consider here. Of course, the transition in the brain is closely linked to social and psychological transitions. More broadly, the teenage years are a transition from childhood to adulthood. Within the overall transition, there are, of course, many smaller transitions. There is the move from one school to another, the changing relationship with close adults, living away from home and so on. The shift from being a child to being a mature individual is a long and complicated process. Because of this, the young person can be both immature and mature at the same time. One of my constant refrains when I talk to parents is: "Inside every teenager there is both a child and an adult".

This duality is frequently reflected in their behaviour. At one time, the teenager will act in a mature and responsible manner, taking decisions and managing day-to-day activities without adult involvement. However, at another time, the young person will behave like a needy child, seeking help and guidance. This can be very frustrating for adults, but it is a natural part of the transition process.

The key element for someone undergoing any transition is uncertainty about whether they are in one state or another. It is this uncertainty that helps to explain many of the behaviours that are typical of the teenage years. Although, as I have said, the uncertainty is also a function of the changes in the brain. The psychological and the neurological combine together to create this stage of life. Transitions have a number of characteristics, including anxiety about the future, excitement about what is to come, and a sense of regret or loss due to the move away from something that is safe and familiar.

Transition creates a world of questions and challenges. It is hard for adults to make the gradual change in how they respond to a young person. There is little consistency – one minute you are facing a child, and the next there is a person who wants to be grown up. Everyone wants to know where they stand and what is expected of them. Yet this is not always possible. Parents and teachers are never quite sure how to treat the young person during these years. It is difficult for the adult to know how much autonomy to allow and how much to expect of the teenager.

Transition is tricky for the young person, too. What is reasonable to expect from the adults around you? On the one hand, the teenager wants to be treated as a responsible person, but that can also be scary. Being looked after and having things done for you is safe and comforting. Add to that the swings of emotion resulting from hormone variation, it will be clear that transitions can be challenging for all concerned.

SOCIAL AND HISTORICAL CHANGE

One factor that has a profound influence on the type of transition experienced by the young person is the social context in which they are growing up. The world that surrounds the teenager today is completely different from the world as it was – say – in the 1980s or 1990s. It is important to keep in mind that the teenager today was born sometime after the year 2005. Since then, there has been so much change it is hard to describe it all. From the banking crisis in 2008 to the years of "austerity" in the 2010s, to Brexit and the pandemic, the world for teenagers is a different place.

There are a number of topics that might be considered under the heading of social change. This could include the family, the world of school and education, entry into the labour market, the financial rules and regulations that apply to those over 16, the general economic situation that affects everyone in the UK, the growth and the importance of the internet and social media. All these factors and many others impact on young people.

In addition to these broad social changes, there are other shifts that reflect changing attitudes to social issues. Examples here include attitudes to race and ethnicity, questions of gender and transitioning, relationships between the sexes, awareness of sexual harassment and sexual exploitation and so on. It is tempting for adults to judge young people according to their own experiences. These experiences lead to beliefs and opinions that will not necessarily accord with what young people believe today.

This is a good place to note that the brain and the environment interact in shaping a young person's development. There are many different features of the environment that are significant here. What we have just outlined refers to the social changes that have occurred leading to different experiences for different generations. In addition to these factors, there are elements of the environment that also impact on human development. As one example, we have learnt that poverty and deprivation have an influence on the brain, especially during the sensitive period of the teenage years. The greater the poverty, the longer the brain takes to come to full maturity.

The actual place where a young person grows up has an influence, too. Whether you grow up in a rural or urban environment will play a part in determining the route to maturity. A good example of this is the fact that the availability of public transport in rural areas affects life chances. Research has shown that, where public transport is scarce, and where young people live far from sexual health services, there are higher rates of teenage pregnancy.

Other studies indicate that parents behave differently towards their teenagers depending on whether they live in safe or unsafe neighbourhoods. In unsafe environments, parenting tends to be more restrictive and controlling. In addition, standards of housing affect health outcomes, so that the poorer the housing, the more likelihood of health risks such as obesity or other long-term health conditions. There are many such examples illustrating the fact that both place and time are key determinants of human development.

TIMING OF LIFE EVENTS

This is an important notion that highlights another factor that influences teenage development. We speak of life events as those things that occur to change or affect the way development occurs. Life events can be assessed according to the degree of stress associated with them. Where teenagers are concerned, this life stage inevitably involves a series of life events, some of them more stressful than others.

The occurrence of puberty combined with a move to a new school is a good example of this. Of course, many people manage this perfectly well. However, if an additional life event occurs, something like a bereavement or family breakdown, then this may become more problematic. There have been many studies on the impact of life events on the stress levels of individuals. Broadly, the more life events that impact on the individual, the more stress is experienced.

Where teenagers are concerned, this is highly significant. Firstly, because this is a period of major change in the brain, and secondly, because the very nature of transition means that change is inevitable. These two factors tell us that the timing of events is especially important. Where life events occur together, there is more possibility of stress. Where life events are spaced out, things are likely to be easier for a teenager to manage during this stage of life.

AGENCY

Agency refers to an individual's ability to manage their own development. Many adults assume that teenagers are primarily influenced by family, school, friends and the neighbourhood. The idea that the young person is an "active agent" in shaping his or her development is a novel thought. Yet, a moment's thought will show how this works.

Imagine a morning in the home of a typical teenager. Even before she or he leaves the house to go to school, a number of decisions have to be made. How to manage and prepare for the day? What to say to parents who ask questions about what is happening after school? How to respond to social media posts? This has sometimes been described as the young person navigating a way through the everyday decisions that have to be taken. At every moment, the individual is shaping their own life in ways that adults rarely recognize.

There are, of course, limits to agency. Some of these are structural, to do with the way power and influence operate in the family or in the community, and some limits are to do with the life events I have already described. Time and place may also be limiting factors. In the case of the pandemic and subsequent lockdowns, this would have had a clear impact on some young people's education and the options that were available at the time.

Nonetheless, a recognition of the place of agency is critical in understanding adolescent development. Research into what is known as information management provides a good example of agency. This refers to the way an individual manages the flow of information towards other people. Let us assume that a 15-year-old has done badly on a piece of schoolwork. She gets feedback from the teacher, but what then? Does she tell her parents, or does she keep this information to herself? This decision involves information management.

She will make a decision as to what to do in this situation. She will navigate her way through this particular event, and will learn to manage the consequences. This is a simple example, but this process applies to a multitude of situations that take place every day. Studies of information management have shown that young people have complex and sophisticated rules in place for making these decisions. They will consider many factors when deciding what to tell and what to hold back. An understanding of how agency works for teenagers can make all the difference in determining the quality of relationships between the generations.

RESILIENCE

I am going to end this chapter with a short note on resilience. The question of how to develop or enhance resilience in young people is a critical one. When we speak of resilience, we mean an ability to overcome hurdles or challenges. The word originates from the Latin, meaning the ability to bounce back. In order to understand resilience, we have to consider both risk and protective factors. Risk factors include aspects of the individual, such as personality and temperament, the role of the family and especially parenting practices, and then community factors such as housing, schools and other resources.

Protective factors are, of course, the mirror image of the risk factors just mentioned. All these variables can represent both risk and protection. In order to understand resilience, we should note that it comes down to the balance of risk and protective factors. The more risk factors there are, the greater threat to resilience. The more protective factors there are, the greater likelihood of a resilient response to adversity.

An additional risk factor that is, of course, at the heart of this book, is the way the brain undergoes the restructuring that I have described. The amount of restructuring of the brain due to pruning, and the variation in hormone levels on a day-to-day basis, are two obvious elements of the changing brain that are relevant here. It is hard to estimate quite what level of risk these changes to the brain represent. This is primarily due to the fact that there are such wide individual differences, and our capacity to measure all aspects of the brain is still limited.

This can be illustrated by thinking about physical puberty, something I will discuss in the next chapter. We know that there are very wide individual differences in the timing of puberty. Some young people can start early, when they are aged 9 or 10, while others do not begin puberty until they are 13 or 14. All this is perfectly normal. However, whether these differences represent a risk depends on all the other factors occurring at the same time. It is here that the timing of life events is so critical.

A number of the topics I have covered in this chapter are pertinent in considering resilience. In the first place, the transition from child to adult involves a multitude of challenges, and the way these are responded to and the support the young person receives, will make a difference to resilience. The type of life event is important, too. The most damaging life events are those that are continuous, taking place over a long period of time. An example of this would be chronic parental conflict. Events that are single, and only happen once, are less likely to create a high level of risk.

It is interesting to consider what resilience means in the context of brain development. I have noted that some aspects of the changes in the brain may create risk. However, it seems obvious that the resilient individual would need input from the prefrontal cortex in order to make decisions, recognize risks and consider consequences. This leads to questions concerning the notion of healthy brain development. By this, I mean the factors that encourage the maturation of this part of the brain. I will have more to say about healthy brain development in the last chapter of the book.

CONCLUSION

In this chapter, I have set out some key themes that impact on development through the teenage years. I have noted the fact that this stage represents a major transition in the life course. It is not too much to say that this is probably one of the most significant transitions that has to be negotiated by any individual during their life. Moving from the status of child to that of an adult involves a remarkable process of adaptation, and yet it is one that we rarely recognize as having such significance. Most adults have completely forgotten this stage, and observe with amazement their own teenagers as they attempt to adjust to the challenges of adolescence.

One of the remarkable aspects of this is that the changes in the brain are completely invisible. While we can all witness the changes to the body of a young teenager, we have no idea what is happening inside the head. It is only recently that we have learnt how significant these processes are, and how much they impact on the young person's behaviour and development. It is for this reason that I hope the information in this book will make a difference to the way adults manage relationships with the young people in their lives.

FURTHER READING

Carey, C (2020) *"What's my teenager thinking?: practical psychology for modern parents"*. Penguin Random House. London.

Coleman J (2011) "The nature of adolescence: 4th Edition". Routledge. Abingdon, Oxon.

Coleman, J (2018) *Why won't my teenager talk to me?: 2nd Edition*". Routledge. Abingdon, Oxon.

Coleman, J and Hagell, A (2007) "*Adolescence: risk and resilience*". John Wiley. Chichester.

Steinberg, L (2015) "*The age of opportunity: lessons from the new science of adolescence*". Mariner Books. New York.

3

RAGING HORMONES

INTRODUCTION

One well-known feature of the teenage years is the fact that hormones are all over the place. Caricatures of teenagers almost always include some reference to hormones. That is why I have called this chapter "Raging hormones". Most people think that when we speak of "raging hormones", we are talking primarily about the sex hormones. These hormones have a major role to play. However, they are not the only hormones that impact on the teenager. I will consider some of the other hormones throughout the course of this chapter.

In the last few years, as a result of research on the brain, we have learnt an enormous amount more about hormones. There are dozens of hormones in our bodies, but also in our brains. These hormones have a profound effect on all of us. In this chapter, I will tell you a little about the most important of these. I will also show how these hormones play a part in the story of the teenage brain.

As part of this chapter, I want also to consider the question of risk and risk-taking. For many years, it was believed that the main reason young people engaged in risky behaviour was because of their hormones. Too much testosterone in boys was seen as the major factor encouraging risk-taking. However, as we have learnt more about the brain, this picture has changed. In this chapter, I will review the evidence on this subject and I will also consider some well-known risky behaviours such as the use of alcohol and drugs.

DOI: 10.4324/9781003331728-3

PUBERTY

I want to start with puberty, the event that heralds the arrival of adolescence. Readers will be aware of the major sex hormones – these are testosterone, estrogen and progesterone. These hormones are produced in the ovaries for females and in the testes for males. They are the main reproductive hormones and are responsible for the onset of puberty, as well as pregnancy, menstruation, sex drive and many other aspects of sexuality.

Young people experience significant physical, psychological and behavioural changes as they mature from a child to an adult. Apart from the early years of infancy, the physical changes of adolescence represent our second fastest period of development. The two or three years of pubertal development include a physical growth spurt, maturing of the reproductive organs, and the development of secondary sex characteristics and the start of periods (menarche) in girls.

There is wide individual variation in the timing of the start and completion of puberty. Often, when people consider what puberty means, they think of girls beginning to menstruate or boys' voices deepening and "breaking". But these are only two of the signs of a major process of change within the body that can take place at any time between the ages of approximately nine and 14.

Some key features of puberty are as follows:

- The various changes associated with puberty will last about two years.
- Puberty generally starts 12 to 18 months earlier for girls than it does for boys.
- In Britain today, the average age for a girl to start menstruating is 11 years and 10 months old. However, 20% will start when they are still in primary school.
- Between 1900 and 1960, the average age at which children started puberty decreased by about one month per decade. Most commentators put this down to better nutrition and improved health care.

- Since then, there has been a smaller amount of change, although evidence is not entirely consistent on this question.
- There are many other physical changes associated with puberty, including changes in the composition of the blood, increasing size of the lungs and heart, and so on.
- Although many of the changes associated with sexual maturation are apparent, emotional changes, which are less obvious, can have a significant impact, too.

It should be emphasized that the age at which young people start puberty is highly variable – it can happen as early as 9 years old or as late as age 14 (and indeed later for some). All this is to be expected and has no implications for later sexual development. But "fitting in" usually matters a great deal to young people. Few want to stand out from the crowd.

Being out of step is sometimes known as being "off-time". When others around you are changing and your body remains child-like, it can be hard. Puberty can therefore be a painful process in this respect, with young people worrying about the pace of change (i.e., nothing is happening or it's all happening at once).

Starting puberty either extremely early or late can cause a lot of anxiety for young people, and for their parents or carers. It is important for adults to know that none of these experiences will necessarily have lasting effects. What is critical is that adults understand how variable the experience of puberty can be. Parents and carers should then be able to provide the necessary information and support for young people who go through puberty outside of the expected age range.

One of the interesting questions is how physical puberty is related to the changes in the brain that were outlined in the previous chapter. So far, research has not given a clear answer on this issue. However, this does matter. As one example, we know that those who come to puberty later than others may struggle with their schoolwork. If that is the case, then delays in brain development could be the explanation. This is one important focus for future research.

HORMONES

In the first chapter, I mentioned the fact that, during the teenage years, there is a marked variation in the level of hormones in the brain. This means that emotion regulation is harder, and it is part of the explanation for mood swings and the flip-flop of emotions. As I have said, there are dozens of hormones that circulate both in our bodies and in our brains. I will describe a few of the ones that are most important for teenage brain development.

The first hormone to mention is **cortisol**. This is one of the key stress hormones, along with adrenaline. Cortisol is released in the brain when we are anxious, stressed or vulnerable. On a short-term basis, cortisol can be useful. When we are under threat, this is the hormone that prepares our body to respond appropriately. This is the famous "fight or flight" response. However, too much cortisol has a detrimental effect, and leads to poor functioning.

The next hormone to consider is **serotonin**. This is the hormone that is released when we are happy, relaxed or at ease. This is the hormone that helps keep our mood steady. Low levels of serotonin can be a factor in low mood or depression. Variation in serotonin levels may play a part in leaving young people at the mercy of feelings of sadness or misery. Teenagers may have extreme reactions to minor setbacks. Common difficulties may lead to the belief that "the end of the world has arrived". Such catastrophic reactions are related to levels of serotonin which affect the amygdala and other sites in the brain.

The third hormone to discuss here is **dopamine**. This is commonly known as the reward hormone. We have learnt that there is more dopamine in the teenage brain than in the adult brain. There are also more dopamine receptors in the brain during these years, and this has a profound effect on behaviour. Readers may have heard people speaking of a "dopamine rush". Because dopamine is a hormone that is especially active in the brain during the teenage years, it can lead to a sensitivity to rewards, as well as motivation to seek rewards.

Finally, I will mention **melatonin**. This is the hormone that makes us feel sleepy and signals that it is time to go to bed. As a result of research on the brain, we have learnt that melatonin is released later at night in young people than it is for adults. This means that it is harder for many teenagers to get to sleep, and this has implications for the amount of sleep that teenagers are getting on school nights. Sleep is extremely important for all of us, but it is particularly important for teenagers. I will deal with this in greater detail in Chapter 6.

SITES OF THE BRAIN

In talking about the brain, I have mentioned the amygdala. This is the predominant site that processes and manages our emotions. However, the brain is extremely complex and many sites play a part in determining our moods and emotions. The amygdala itself is part of a larger system known as the limbic system. It is also important to remember that the brain is in two halves – two hemispheres. Each of the sites exists in both hemispheres, so each site is mirrored on both sides of the brain.

This raises the question as to how the two halves of the brain work together. I mentioned the notion of connectivity in Chapter 1. This refers to the structures that allow the two halves of the brain to be coordinated. To think about this gives you an idea of how immensely complex the working of the brain must be. The bridge in the middle of the brain that makes this connectivity possible is called the **corpus callosum**. One of the ways we measure maturity in the brain is by seeing how this bridge gradually becomes more sophisticated and elaborate as the young person grows older.

Another part of the brain that is important to mention here is that associated with reward processing. In years gone by, before scanning was available, scientists believed that there was a reward centre in the brain. This notion was based on research on animals. It was a great surprise when results from scanning confirmed this belief. It turns out that there is, indeed, a site in the human brain that processes rewards. This site, known as the **nucleus accumbens**, can be seen to become especially active and aroused when rewards are presented, or even imagined.

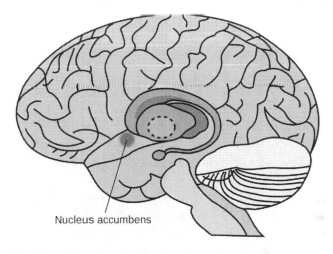

Nucleus accumbens

Figure 3.1 The nucleus accumbens

In addition to connectivity across the two halves of the brain, there is also the question of how the sites are coordinated. So, for example, it is important to consider how the prefrontal cortex is networked with the sites that process emotions. This is pertinent, since the stronger the networks between these two areas of the brain, the more likely it is that the individual will be able to manage and control the hormones that activate emotional behaviour. It is probable that, during the teenage years, the networks that connect the cortex and the amygdala will gradually strengthen. While these networks remain immature, the individual may struggle to control emotions. As the networks become more mature, this process becomes easier, and more adult behaviour becomes possible.

STRESS

When there is a discussion of stress, the phrase "fight or flight" is often mentioned. In essence, the brain releases two main chemical messengers in response to the presence of a stressor. These chemicals prepare the body to respond in a way that will protect the individual from threat. In other words, these substances in the body enable the individual to respond to danger by raising the heart rate, increasing oxygen levels, redirecting blood to the muscles and so on.

These responses are part of our primitive history when we lived in times of ever-present danger. Today, threats are likely to be different, and the "fight or flight" response may not necessarily be appropriate. For teenagers, threats may come in many forms such as anxiety about tests and exams, conflict with parents, rejection within the peer group, not receiving many likes on social media, and many other social circumstances.

We have learnt a considerable amount about how stress affects the teenage brain. In particular, we know that the brains of young people do not respond in the same way to stress as adult brains. Stress affects the amygdala and other areas of the brain to do with the processing of emotion. The teenage amygdala has less capacity to deal with fear and anger, thus leading to more extreme or inappropriate responses to these emotions. The emotions of worry, anxiety and stress are all associated with levels of cortisol in the brain. Research has shown that cortisol levels are somewhat higher in adolescence than in adulthood.

A different perspective on stress comes from studies of self-control. This evidence comes from examples of placing young people in situations in which a good decision involves holding back until more information is available. When teenagers are calm and relaxed, they show just as much self-control as adults. However, under conditions of stress or other strong emotions, the self-control of a teenager deteriorates. This can lead to poor decision-making. Thus, it is clear that young people can think about consequences in some situations, but not in all situations. We will explore this issue in greater detail in the next section.

RISKY BEHAVIOUR

Thinking about consequences leads us neatly into a discussion of risk and risk-taking. This is a question that has a long history in the study of adolescence. From the time that the idea of "the teenager" came to public notice, from the 1940s onwards, risk-taking was considered to be a key element of teenage behaviour. This led to a big debate about whether this idea was unfair to young people. Many argued that not all teenagers take risks and that, furthermore, some risk-taking may be necessary in order to explore the world and experiment with what is safe and what is harmful.

This is where the study of the brain comes in. You will remember that in Chapter 1 I mentioned that the brain matures from back to front. This means that the amygdala, part of the limbic system in the central area of the brain, may mature earlier than the prefrontal cortex. After the advent of scanning (say, from the years 2000 to 2010), research was appearing that suggested this was the reason that young people are risk-takers. If the areas of the brain to do with thinking, reasoning and problem-solving are maturing more slowly than sites to do with emotion and sensation, that may explain why young people find it hard to consider whether their behaviour is safe or unsafe. In other words, here is the reason why young people take risks without fully considering the consequences of their actions.

In recent years scientists have become much more cautious about this explanation. As more studies have been published, it has become apparent that early conclusions were premature. Extensive studies have shown very large differences between individuals. While in some the brain may mature from back to front, this is not the case for everyone. And then, in addition, it should be obvious that many factors affect risk-taking. The level of hormones in the brain has an impact and the brain and the environment interact, so that social factors will also influence risk-taking.

Earlier in this chapter, I mentioned the hormone dopamine. This is the reward hormone, and there is more dopamine in the teenage brain than in the adult brain. For some young people, at some points in time, higher levels of dopamine may lead to a push for rewards and exciting experiences. This push may easily encourage risky behaviour.

We should also note the impact of social factors, such as the influence of other members of the family. Parents and older siblings may act as role models and thereby offer examples of certain types of risky behaviour. We also know that the peer group plays a part here, too. I will discuss this in greater detail in Chapter 5. However, at this point, it is important to note that studies clearly show higher levels of risk-taking when peers are present.

One interesting focus of recent research has been an attempt to distinguish between what are called "hot" and "cold" situations. This links with what I was saying about self-control and being able to hold back before taking action. What does this mean? The distinction refers to the amount of emotion present in the situation. So, for example, a "hot" situation may be one where the young person is at a party, surrounded by friends, or one where the stakes are high in terms of relationships or attractive rewards. Brain imaging shows that areas of the brain, such as the amygdala, are more active in such situations. In these circumstances, it is harder to engage the prefrontal cortex and thus avoid risky behaviour.

I want to make one final point about risk. I like to use the term "trainee adult" when describing a teenager. After all, there are many situations where individuals can be described as trainees. So, for example, in a work setting, individuals at the start of their placement are trainees. In such circumstances, we do not expect them to get everything right the first time. We allow the trainee to make some mistakes, as this is part of the learning process. And, I would argue, the same could be said for the teenager. Adults should be able to take this into account. So, when a young person appears to get some-thing wrong, it is important to "cut them some slack". They won't get everything right first time. That is fine, as it is all part of the process of growing up and learning how to be an adult.

REWARD PROCESSING

It is time now to move on to consider the question of rewards. As I noted, dopamine is known as the reward hormone, and there is more of this in the teenage brain. It is for this reason that there has been a strong focus on the topic of rewards and reward processing in recent research. Dopamine has two functions. On the one hand, it encourages behaviour that may lead to a reward or a sensation of pleasure. It also has a separate role, in that dopamine is released following a reward, causing a feeling of well-being and satisfaction.

Many studies, using both animal and human subjects, have shown a peak level of the release of dopamine during the adolescent period. This means that young people are more sensitive to the potential rewards that come from the use of social media, and from using drugs, going to parties, or eating fast food and sugary snacks. This finding has big implications for understanding teenage behaviour. It also has relevance if we want to identify the things that are most likely to motivate young people, whether that is in the classroom or at home.

I will mention a couple of studies here that illustrate this point. The first makes use of "The Wheel of Fortune" game. Here, participants spin the wheel, as in roulette, and the number the wheel lands on determines the level of reward. Both adults and young people take part while their brains are being scanned. The results indicate that teenagers show more activity in the reward areas of the brain than adults when they win.

Another similar study has the participants seeing three cues on a screen. Each cue is associated with a different level of reward. The goal is to identify the cue that gives the highest level of reward. The earnings associated with each cue are then shown on the screen. Participants can then get feedback on how much reward they will receive. The results demonstrate that areas in the brain associated with reward are activated to a greater degree in adolescents than in other age groups. Also of interest is the fact that these areas continue to show a higher level of activation for a longer period after reward in the teenage participants.

These findings have great significance. The knowledge we now have about the importance of rewards for young people should change the way adults engage with this generation. Why? Because we know that, in the relationships between adults and young people, there tends to be less focus on reward and more focus on nagging, complaints and general negative feedback. Once adults recognize how sensitive teenagers are to reward, a shift in behaviour becomes possible. This is relevant as much to the school setting as it is to the home.

Some may say, what rewards? Of course, rewards should be age appropriate. What may be rewarding for a 12-year-old will not be suitable for a 16-year-old. Rewards associated with consumer behaviour, whether money, toys, gadgets or similar things, should be avoided. The most powerful rewards are praise, recognition, support and the giving of appropriate responsibility. There will be more on this topic in the final chapter.

DRUGS AND ALCOHOL

I want to say something about these topics as they link closely with the notion of risk and reward. When I give webinars about the teenage brain, one of the most common questions I get has to do with the use of alcohol, cannabis or other drugs. Participants usually want to know whether the presence of particular hormones in the teenage brain explains why some teenagers are especially attracted to the use of substances. Naturally, this leads to the question of what we can do about addiction or over-use of drugs and alcohol.

First, I will give a quick outline of the effects of alcohol on the brain. Of course, the impact will depend on how much the individual is drinking. In addition, we know that, again, there are individual differences in alcohol tolerance. In general, we can say that alcohol affects three key areas of the brain – the frontal areas, the hippocampus and the cerebellum. The frontal areas have to do with thinking and reasoning, the hippocampus is where memories are processed, and the cerebellum is the area controlling physical movement.

Why is drinking alcohol appealing, especially to young people? The immediate impact is that alcohol impacts the hormones to do with anxiety and stress, so that drinking leads to disinhibition and a greater sense of ease in social situations. In addition to this, alcohol impacts the release of dopamine, inducing a sense of well-being. However, as with all addictive substances, as time goes on more alcohol is needed to keep up the dopaminergic effect.

Drinking is almost a rite of passage for young people, so the more parents and schools can introduce good alcohol education, the better. For the great majority of teenagers, getting drunk a few times at parties or similar events is considered the norm. Helping teenagers to understand the effects of alcohol, as well as the long-term outcomes of heavy drinking, can only be for the good.

Cannabis is another substance that is commonly in use among this age group. We now know that THC is the psychoactive agent that leads to the perception of relaxation, pleasure and even euphoria. Experiences such as listening to music are enhanced and intensified. Anxiety is usually decreased, but sometimes it can be increased and can cause depression or low mood. The important thing to note is that the amount of THC varies greatly in different types of cannabis. There are many forms of cannabis now available. The higher the amount of THC, the greater the psychoactive impact. Higher levels of THC lead to more intense levels of pleasure, but also to less inhibition.

The worry about cannabis is that, frequently, young people do not know the level of THC in the substances they are using. High levels of THC may lead people to experience lower inhibition, causing troubling behaviours such as aggression or even violence. We have also learnt that frequent cannabis use may be a precursor to mental health problems. Using cannabis three times or more in a week is undoubtedly a risk factor for psychotic illness. The more information that is available about cannabis for adults and young people, the better.

Lastly in this section, I will briefly mention other drugs, such as ecstasy, cocaine and heroin. These substances have similar effects on the brain as cannabis and alcohol, but the impact is often greater and more intense. Such substances are, in addition, more likely to be addictive. This is because the effect on the hormones in the brain is more powerful, leading to longer-lasting changes. As one example, studies of the use of ecstasy show that this drug affects every area of the brain and has a particular impact on the production of serotonin.

Teenagers process cocaine and other hard drugs differently from adults. This is partly because the brain is still maturing during the adolescent stage. In addition, drugs such as cocaine are stimulants, and these substances lead to the release of a greater amount of dopamine in the adolescent brain. Furthermore, the impact is especially powerful in those areas of the brain that process rewards, such as the nucleus accumbens, where habits are easily formed. Scientists have called the results on these sites in the brain "a biochemical express lane". This indicates that these substances act faster and for longer on the teenage brain than on the adult brain.

CONCLUSION

In this chapter, I have shown some of the ways in which hormones act in the teenage brain. There are dozens of hormones in our brains and in our bodies. However, we have learnt that particular hormones play a big part in the brain during this period of rapid change. Hormones such as dopamine, serotonin and cortisol are of special importance. I have described how hormones impact on the process of puberty, and I have covered some of the key findings concerning risky behaviour and the processing of rewards. I concluded the chapter with a short section on drugs and alcohol, since I believe the use of these substances offers an example of how hormones and risky behaviour work together. Many of these issues will make an appearance in other chapters, as we move on to consider the peer group, sleep and mental health.

FURTHER READING

Barrett, L F (2020) *"Seven and a half lessons about the brain"*. Picador. London.

Coleman, J (2011) *"The nature of adolescence: 4th Edition"*. Routledge. Abingdon, Oxon.

Galvan, A (2017) *"The neuroscience of adolescence"*. Cambridge University Press. Cambridge.

Morgan, N (2005) *"Blame my brain: the amazing teenage brain revealed: 2nd Edition"*. Walker Books. London.

4

LEARNING, LEARNING, LEARNING

INTRODUCTION

Many years ago, Professor Michael Rutter and colleagues wrote a book called *Fifteen Thousand Hours* (1979). They used this title as they concluded that the average teenager would spend approximately this number of hours in school over the course of their time in secondary education. It is assumed that, during this period the essential element of activity will be learning. Although a proportion of the time in school will not necessarily be devoted to learning, but to managing relationships with peers and adults, learning is nonetheless at the heart of the school experience.

There is no doubt that the demands of school weigh heavily on the shoulders of most teenagers. In my own experience, young people tell me that they see school as the most stressful feature of their lives. When asked what is most stressful about being a teenager they respond: "Tests, homework, exams, pressure from teachers, pressure from parents, learning, learning".

Our growing knowledge of the brain has helped us to understand what underpins the development of learning. In earlier times, it was assumed that learning occurs as a result of good teaching. It was assumed that the increased knowledge and skills that come about as young people move through the school years are largely due to the quality of teaching and the inherent potential of the individual student.

DOI: 10.4324/9781003331728-4

We now know that the changes in the brain during these years make possible improvements in thinking, reasoning and problem-solving. These improvements are an essential component of learning. Without these skills, it would not be possible to tackle the curriculum in Key Stages 3 and 4. It is time now to look more closely at how learning develops during the teenage years.

How LEARNING TAKES PLACE

Chapter 1 outlined some basic information about the brain. I noted that neurons are connected to each other in patterns and networks. The brain operates by sending impulses along nerve pathways. I mentioned the role of synapses, the tiny gaps between neurons. These synapses play a critical role, as they either facilitate or hinder the continuing passage of the impulse around the brain. Information that comes into the brain is stored temporarily in short-term memory – in the hippocampus and associated structures. If the information matches with existing memories, it is discarded. On the other hand, if the information is new, it is sent out to various regions in the brain to be processed and stored for future use.

The brain is designed to attend to new information. This is essentially what learning is. The more activity there is between neurons, the stronger the synapse. One of my teachers at university (Professor Don Hebb) coined the phrase: *"What fires together, wires together"*. This refers to the fact that the more particular neurons activate together, the more likely it is that learning will take place.

The more a piece of information is repeated or relearned, the stronger the synapse becomes. Some have described this as being like a path through a meadow. The more you walk through the long grass, the clearer and more defined the path becomes.

Two words are useful here. They are "frequency" and "recency". The more frequent and the more recent our learning, the stronger the likelihood that this learning will be successful. To put it another way, if we learn something often, and if we learn it within a short period of time, the probability is greater that this learning will become embedded.

The process by which learning takes place is known as long-term potentiation (LTP). What does this mean? If the connections between the neurons become strengthened and entrenched, then it is said that long-term potentiation has taken place. In other words, there is a greater possibility that these connections will work again next time. In order for this to happen, both sides of the synapse have to be "on". The receptors on both sides of the synapse have to be in receptive mode.

During the process of learning, the synapse becomes stronger and stronger, which, in turn, causes a bigger response in the neuron that has been activated. It is a fascinating thought that, if you are learning any of this as you read, you will be building new receptors. Whenever you are learning something new, additional receptors are added to the synapse. Following learning, and over the next time period, the synapse will be cemented into a stronger form, as shown in Figure 4.1.

I previously pointed out that there are both "on" and "off" receptors in the brain. What if the receptor on either side of the synapse is "off"? This is the process by which the brain manages the flow of information. As you can imagine, at any one moment the brain is flooded with new sensory input, as well as messages from various organs, muscles

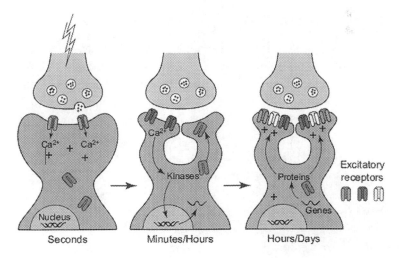

Figure 4.1 New receptors are added to synapses during learning

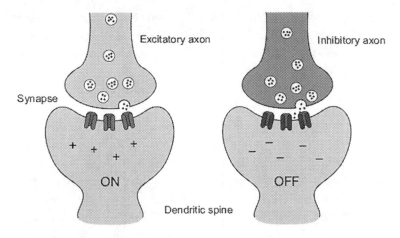

Figure 4.2 Inhibition and the on/off mechanism

and glands that control our hormones. The brain needs to screen out some information, otherwise it would be overwhelmed. This is the function of the receptors that inhibit the flow of information around the brain. The on/off mechanism is shown in Figure 4.2.

PRUNING AND PLASTICITY

One of the features of brain development in the teenage years is the process of pruning. Pruning refers to the process of reducing the volume of grey matter in the brain. I pointed out in Chapter 1 that this is a hugely significant feature of the changes taking place at this time. An over-production of neurons at the end of childhood means that the brain has too many neurons and too many networks. These have to be reduced for good functioning. Connections between neurons that are no longer needed are allowed to die away, while those that are of value become embedded. Some have called this process "neural Darwinism", since it is only the "fittest" that survive. In this sense, "fittest" means those that are most used.

It is a strange thought that some parts of the brain actually reduce during this stage. In this case, one could say that less means more!

Another way of putting it is to say that the brain becomes a "leaner, meaner machine". In essence, the brain becomes more efficient. I should also note that the brain does not only consist of grey matter. While the grey matter clusters around the outside of the cortex, there is white matter in the centre of the cortex to be taken into account. It is the white matter where most of the connections between neurons lie. This is the part of the brain that actually increases in size during

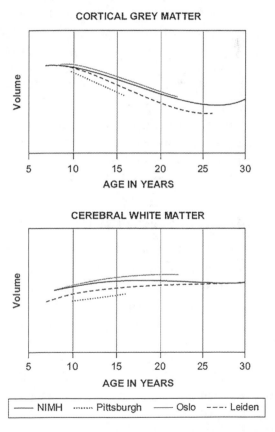

Figure 4.3 Two graphs showing change in white and grey matter (Art No. 20 from list of illustrations).

Source: Mills, K A, et al. (2016).

the teenage years. So, while we have a reduction in grey matter, at the same time, other areas of the brain are growing.

Finally in this section, I want to say something about what is known as **brain plasticity**. This is a term used to describe the capacity of the brain to repair itself. This may be following a bad accident, or it may be due to illness or disease. However, plasticity also refers to the adaptability of the brain as it responds to pruning, and other changes that follow on from this. Plasticity of the brain during the teenage years allows for increased learning capacity. The connectivity between the two hemispheres develops and the brain responds to these changes, becoming a better learning machine. Adolescence is one of those stages of life where there is truly a rapid development of learning capacity.

Because there is so much change taking place, it is reasonable to see this stage of life as a "sensitive period" as far as the brain is concerned. This means that what happens during this period really matters. Learning experiences during the teenage years have long-term implications for later development. It also means that, even when things have not gone well during the primary school years, there is an important window of opportunity during adolescence.

IS THERE A DIFFERENCE BETWEEN LEARNING AND MEMORY?

Most writers make little distinction between these two ideas. However, it seems important to explore this a bit further. In the first instance, one could say that memory is a **capacity** − in other words, a resource or a strength, something you can draw on. On the other hand, learning is a **process**. Learning is something that takes place in time, leading to a change in the brain. Furthermore, memory is essentially dependent on the capabilities of the brain. Learning, on the other hand, is influenced by a wider range of factors, such as family, the school environment and the teacher. Motivation and interest in the subject make a difference, too.

Let us look at some examples. If you were learning a poem, as one instance, you could say that you were memorizing it, or you were learning it. In this case, the two words are interchangeable. However, you would not say that someone was memorizing how to drive. You would say they were learning to drive. A trainee chef would not be memorizing how to cook. Such a person would be learning how to cook. Of course, they might be memorizing a recipe, which illustrates the point. In the case of activities that involve a range of skills, it is more usual to refer to the process as learning. When it is a case of rote learning, we are more likely to use the word memory. There is the conundrum. I have just used the words learning and memory in the same sentence! How can we tell them apart?

Does this matter? It is important for our purposes, since different areas of the brain are likely to be involved in the different processes. As an example, there is one type of memory that refers to our ability to recall facts and bring events and information into consciousness. This aspect of memory is most likely to be associated with the hippocampus and associated brain structures. Another type of memory refers to habits and routines linked to performance, such as riding a bicycle. Here, we are carrying out an activity without much effort or thought. These types of memories are likely to be located in areas such as the spinal cord and the cerebellum.

We can now see that, where school learning is concerned, it is probable that the first type of memory is the one that is most engaged. This will help us when we look at the sites in the brain that show changes following various cognitive activities.

EXECUTIVE FUNCTION

Executive function is one of the key concepts used for understanding the increasing the capacity of the brain during the teenage years. Executive function is the term used to describe certain processes that underlie learning. This is a field of study that has aroused great interest in the last decade or so. This is because it can be shown that executive function is closely related to academic performance. There are good studies that indicate that the skills that combine to make up executive function can be used to predict performance on tests and exams in school. This evidence gives us a good pointer to the fact that it is not just good teaching that leads to success in the classroom. What is happening in the brain is making a vital contribution as well.

There are generally considered to be four elements that make up executive function. These are:

- working memory
- inhibition
- resistance to interference
- flexibility

Next, I am going to explore each of these aspects of executive function in more detail. It is only through an understanding of these four elements that we can fully understand the process of learning in the classroom.

WORKING MEMORY

Working memory refers to our ability to hold a certain amount of information in our attention while we are processing it. This is a key skill, and has been shown to increase gradually from infancy onwards. How much can any of us hold in our memory at any one time? A well-known psychologist, George Miller, once wrote a paper entitled *The magic number seven, plus or minus two*. This is a classic article in social science and refers, of course, to the challenge – what exactly is working memory? What is the maximum number of bits of information that can be held in our active memory at one point in time?

This is significant for our understanding of learning in the teenage years and is a capability that underpins intellectual activity. It is interesting to note that, until recently, this was a capacity that was believed to be fully developed by the end of childhood. Now we know that working memory, among other skills, continues to develop throughout adolescence. Working memory can be measured by varying the amount of time between the presentation of information and the demand to retrieve it. Another way of assessing working memory is to vary the amount of information, rather than the timing. Readers will be familiar with the parlour game of placing a number of items on a tray and giving a certain time for those playing to memorize the objects, and then asking how many can be recalled.

This can be replicated in the laboratory, where the number of objects to be memorized can be varied. In one task, there may be ten objects. This number can then be increased gradually to test working memory at different ages. Studies show that working memory improves during childhood and up to the age of 15. The changes between ages 11 and 15 are more gradual than during childhood.

A different approach to this is to ask the participants to reorganize the material while they memorize it. For example, they may be presented with a string of letters – M, B, I, P, F, R, X, L. In order to memorize these letters, the subject needs to find a way of linking them together. This is a harder task. The individual has to do some work in order to carry out the memory task. This probably involves different parts of the brain. Here, the difference between adults and young people is more marked. Research shows that this skill only develops gradually during the teenage years.

Working memory is an essential skill needed for many of the activities taking place in the classroom. A mathematics or science problem that requires the manipulation of figures or other types of information will be dependent on working memory. Designing schedules or planning activities during the school day, as well as subjects as varied music and language, all utilize working memory.

How does this link with our understanding of the brain? It appears that, during childhood, activities to do with memory are diffused across different regions of the cortex. However, the sites associated with working memory become more developed with age and can do more of the work on their own. In addition, the sites that link the prefrontal cortex with the hippocampus become more mature. All this leads to a slowly improving memory capacity. Interestingly, working memory is not something that is routinely tested in school. Yet, as working memory becomes stronger, learning becomes easier. Should teachers be attending to this aspect of brain development?

INHIBITION

The skill implied here is the ability to stop oneself doing one thing while concentrating on another. In other words, being able to concentrate on a particular task while ignoring other things that might be distracting. This is an essential capacity for learning. In the brain, the ability to activate inhibition depends on the receptors that I mentioned earlier. These are known as the "off" receptors. These are the ones that prevent or inhibit the passage of a message that travels along the nerve fibres.

There are a multitude of ways in which inhibition plays a part in learning. In fact, it would not be possible to pay attention in class without the ability to inhibit stimuli in the surrounding environment. Can you imagine all the things that might be going on in the classroom? You have to screen out the behaviour of other pupils, the things that are going on outside the window and in the corridor, and indeed your own bodily messages such as aches from muscles or feelings of hunger or thirst. In addition, inhibition is essential for learning since new learning often involves un-learning old material. Thirdly, we make assumptions about our environment depending on what is obvious around us. A good example is the belief that the world is round. It looks flat, but we have to inhibit that idea to learn that it is, in fact, round.

Inhibition is not just essential for learning. It plays a major part in the way our brain functions in almost every situation you can imagine. When I explain to students why inhibition is so important, I illustrate this by talking about a railway network. In such a network, you have to have a signalling system otherwise the trains would bump into each other and the network would come to a standstill. Other scientists like to talk about an air-traffic control system, stopping planes from colliding in mid-air. The point is the same. In our brains, there are literally millions of messages being transmitted every second. There has to be a system that allows these messages to be sorted into the ones that matter and the ones that can be halted or put to one side. Inhibition is the process that makes all this possible.

While we know that the skill of inhibition increases with age, there are also individual differences between pupils of the same age.

Thus, some young people struggle with the capacity to inhibit things that are distracting. These young people may find difficulty in concentrating in class, or they may have a problem being able to sit down for long periods. In extreme cases, this leads to a condition known as ADHD (attention deficit hyperactivity disorder). I will have more to say about this condition in Chapter 7.

RESISTANCE TO INTERFERENCE

I have already talked about the capacity to ignore stimuli that are distracting or irrelevant. As I have said, concentration would not be possible without this ability. However, sometimes the distraction is located within the task itself. In this example, the individual has to screen out some aspects of the task in order to find the solution. Reading inhibition provides one illustration of this.

The Stroop test was developed as a way of measuring this ability. The task is simple. An individual is shown a picture of the word RED, and the letters are in red. The task is to name the colour. You may think this is rather easy! However, when the word is GREEN, but the letters are in red, the task becomes more difficult. The areas of the brain needed to perform the Stroop test keep changing and maturing all through the teenage years.

The older the adolescent, the better he or she is at suppressing irrelevant information. In this case, the colour of the lettering is the irrelevant information. This is an excellent means of illustrating resistance to interference. A particular area of the frontal cortex plays a key role here, and as a result of scanning, we can see how this develops with age. Interestingly, this area continues to mature until the early 20s. Even older teenagers struggle with this task, especially if the demands of the task are increased by giving less and less time to make a decision.

FLEXIBILITY

The last of the four elements of executive function is flexibility. Many would argue that this skill is as essential as all the others for learning and memory. Flexibility is needed when we learn new skills. Why? Because, in most situations, learning requires feedback about how we are getting on. Are we doing something correctly, or have we made an error? If we have made an error, then we need to correct it before we can proceed with our learning.

In essence, this is about feedback. The skill of flexibility is determined by whether the individual is paying attention to feedback from errors, or ignoring the feedback and ploughing on. Many studies show that children in primary school have more difficulty taking account of feedback than do those in older age groups. Of course, feedback can come from many different sources. Thinking about this raises questions about feedback from teachers and other adults. How is feedback communicated, and with what accompanying message? Does feedback come with praise, criticism or disinterest? The nature of feedback plays a critical role in assisting or hindering learning.

Flexibility has been measured in the laboratory by creating situations where individuals are required to apply rules in problem-solving. For example, in one such experiment, the task was to respond in a certain way following the presentation of a stimulus, which is a colour. The individual was then told whether the response was right or wrong. Once a participant has been responding correctly for a while, the rule was changed abruptly. The individual then had to use the feedback to work out the new rule. Studies show that the skill of flexibility increases with age.

It appears that feedback which indicates that a mistake has been made leads to activation in two brain areas in the frontal cortex connected to purposeful behaviour. Scientists have called this system the "alarm" system because it becomes active when people make errors. Studies have shown that these areas of the brain are maturing slowly during the teenage years. The learner has to be able to recruit these areas of the brain when solving problems. The ability to recruit them only develops slowly, and is affected by maturation in the later teenage years.

TYPES OF LEARNING

It is time now to consider how our understanding of executive function contributes to useful knowledge about young people. As far as working memory is concerned, it will be obvious that this has its limits. Working memory restricts how much information the individual has at their disposal at any one time. This is demonstrated in our everyday life, as, for example, when we make shopping lists or put a telephone number into our smartphone. We cannot hold more than a certain amount of information in our minds at any one moment. We therefore need to find ways of helping our memory out.

In terms of classroom activity, we can assist students to think about this in order to lighten the load on their working memory. Many young people will face difficulties when having to learn new material. One way of dealing with this is to encourage them to articulate the processes they are using to solve problems. This may be through writing things down, or by documenting the steps taken to arrive at a solution.

Research has demonstrated how this works in the brain. When students are first introduced to a problem, for example a mathematics problem, they tend to use a range of locations in the frontal cortex. With practice, brain activity alters. As students become more familiar with strategies to reduce the load on working memory, shifts can be detected in the brain. When learning processes become more automatic, activity in the frontal cortex is reduced and relocated to different sites in the brain.

Another question that is important for students is how best to learn new material. This is where we can point to the importance of different modes of learning. For many years we have known that learning in more than one mode can enhance memory. This is sometimes known as **multi-modal learning**. What does this mean? If learning involves both visual and verbal elements, there is arousal in different regions of the brain. Where more than one region of the brain is involved, there is a clear advantage for students. An additive effect occurs, so that when more than one brain region is engaged, learning is likely to be more successful.

This leads us to a discussion of **visualization**. Studies show that the process of visualizing an object engages nearly as many sites in the brain as happens when we see the object in front of us. As a result, it will be apparent that the use of mental imagery is a powerful tool in any learning activity. The importance of visualization leads us on to the topic of **vicarious learning**. There has been much discussion in the literature of what are called **mirror neurons**. These are neurons that fire when we observe other people doing things, rather than doing them ourselves.

The interesting thing about these neurons is that they appear to fire in much the same way as they would if we were actually carrying out the behaviour. This means that learning can occur simply through observation. It also underlines the importance of visualization. Simply bringing up an image in our minds has a powerful effect, leading to activity not just in the visual cortex but in the frontal areas as well. All this has profound implications for the learner. Attempts to learn material by simply rehearsing it, using what is known as rote learning, will not be as effective as looking for visual or other links to such material.

In the UK, it is rare to find examples of students being taught study skills. We do not have, in our curriculum, information about topics such as visualization and multi-modal learning. In some countries, study skills are routinely taught to students, so that they learn about the topics I have just described. In my own work with secondary school pupils, I find that the majority are using simple rote learning. They have not been introduced to different methods of learning new material. In my view, the information that I have covered in this chapter could be of great help in schools across the country.

CONCLUSION

Learning and memory are topics of huge importance for young people and for all who work in education. In this chapter, I have shown how our knowledge about the working of the brain when learning takes place has made huge strides in recent years. We now know not just what happens in the brain during the process of learning, but how we can make learning more effective. An important part of this knowledge has to do with executive function. This term applies to the four aspects which are essential for learning: working memory, inhibition, flexibility and resistance to interference.

These have all been illustrated by studies in neuroscience. All four have been shown to be critical elements of cognitive function. They provide the bedrock of skills that underlie new learning during the teenage years. I have also outlined different types of learning, such as visualization and multi-modal learning. Knowledge of these can be used to assist and accelerate the learning process. There is no doubt that one of the major contributions of the science of brain development has been its contribution to our knowledge of learning and memory.

FURTHER READING

Blakemore, S-J (2019) "*Inventing ourselves: the secret life of the teenage brain*". Transworld Publishers/Penguin. London.

Dehaene, S (2020) "*How we learn: the new science of education and the brain*". Penguin. London.

Rutter, M, et al. (1979) "*Fifteen hours: secondary schools and their effects on children*". Open Books. London.

Scott, S (2022) "*The brain: 10 things you should know*". Orion Publishing. London.

Thomas, M, Mareschal, D and Dumontheil, I (Eds.) (2020) "*Educational neuroscience: development across the lifespan*". Routledge. Abingdon, Oxon.

5

THE SOCIAL BRAIN

INTRODUCTION

In this chapter, I am going to explore what is meant by "the social brain". In order to fully understand this aspect of brain function, it is useful to have some knowledge of the role of the peer group for young people. Many years ago, my namesake (J. S. Coleman) wrote a book called *The Adolescent Society*, based on a study in high schools in California, and it has remained a classic in the field. It documented how peer groups function for young people. Coleman made the point that a peer group works as a different society from that of the adults, with different norms and values. In particular, he highlighted the factors that determine popularity and social status. This book demonstrated just how powerful one's peer group can be for this age group.

There are many reasons why peers play such an important role for teenagers. Friendship, support and a forum in which to develop new social skills are all important factors. The changes that young people experience at this age can be puzzling and worrying, and having others going through the same things can be hugely valuable. Another factor has to do with identity development. At a time when questions of identity are foremost in the teenager's mind, being able to test out who you are, who you want to be with, who thinks and feels like you — these are all significant elements of the peer-group experience.

DOI: 10.4324/9781003331728-5

In this chapter, I will outline what is known about the "social brain", and I will describe the ways in which development in this part of the brain affects the behaviour of young people. First, though, I want to provide some background. I will do this by exploring the social world of teenagers. I will consider popularity, conformity, risk-taking and the importance of social media.

POPULARITY AND CONFORMITY

Many studies of teenage peer groups have highlighted the importance of popularity. Peer groups have complex and sophisticated processes by which popularity is determined. In *The Adolescent Society*, J. S. Coleman argued that skill on the sports field affects popularity for boys, and that social success plays the same role for girls. Later studies have identified many other factors which play a role in this process. Different schools and neighbourhoods have a variety of criteria determining popularity. What is certain is that, at this age, how you are viewed by your peers is a major element in your sense of self. I will come on to the role of social media below.

Another topic that has received attention from social scientists is conformity. This is the feature of behaviour that applies to the tendency to "go along with the crowd". It is a common view that, at times, teenagers behave like sheep, dressing in the same way, liking the same things, and generally trying to be as similar to each other as possible. Of course, this is just a stereotype. However, it is the case that young people can be influenced by the opinions of others, especially those in elite or more powerful peer groups.

Conformity in adolescence has been studied by putting young people in situations where they are asked to make a choice or decision where that appears to go against what everyone else in the group is saying. The fascinating thing about the results of these studies is that conformity is not spread equally across all age groups. Thus, the willingness to go along with others reaches a peak around the age of 14. After that, this tendency decreases, so that by 16 or 17, young people are much more able to disagree with the group and to stand up for their own opinion. This is an important finding. It demonstrates that the influence of the peer group is not the same across all ages. As young people mature, they become more resilient, and more able to defend their opinions as individuals.

RISKY BEHAVIOUR

This discussion of conformity links neatly with a consideration of risky behaviour. There has been much debate about the influence of the peer group on risk-taking. As I noted in Chapter 2, this topic was one of the first to be highlighted as the early results of brain imaging became available. Scientists argued that risk-taking could be explained by the fact that the prefrontal cortex matures more slowly than the amygdala. This led to the hormones associated with risk, such as dopamine, being more powerful in influencing behaviour. Later studies have shown that this explanation is too simple, and that many other factors influence risk-taking.

One of these factors is the presence of the peer group. A number of studies have explored this topic. One of the most well-known is the driving study. Here, the participants are asked to take a car round a race track in a driving simulator. The task is to get round the track as fast as possible. The track is littered with obstacles, so some risk-taking is inevitable. When teenagers and adults are alone in the car, there is no difference in risk-taking. However, when the drivers are joined by friends, the difference is striking. In this situation, teenagers are likely to take almost twice as many risks as the adult drivers.

Another factor that may influence risk-taking is the context. As I mentioned in Chapter 3, a distinction has been made between "hot" and "cold" situations. As the reader can imagine, a "hot" situation is one where emotions are running high, or when those involved are having a good time at a party or other similar social situation. In "cold" situations, when individuals have time to think and consider consequences, then, again, there is no difference between adults and young people. In "hot" situations, however, teenagers are more likely to become involved in risky behaviour. It is in these situations that the networks within the brain come into play. The more immature these networks, the more likely it is that behaviour will be impacted by the hormones in the amygdala and associated sites in the brain.

SOCIAL MEDIA

The place of social media in influencing teenage behaviour is a huge topic. In this book, I will only have space to refer to a few aspects of this fascinating subject. In this context, I will briefly outline what needs to be considered in relation to popularity, body image and identity. When considering popularity, I said I would return to the importance of social media. As everyone is aware, social media platforms allow, or even encourage, users to indicate likes in response to posts of various sorts. For teenagers, especially those in the earlier years of puberty, the number of likes received becomes a proxy for popularity.

This then has the potential to cause anxiety if the young person does not receive enough likes to make them feel comfortable. This is especially important, as I say, for those who feel vulnerable and are therefore particularly sensitive to endorsement by their peers. Another feature of the social media arena has to do with the posting of images of the "ideal body". Images posted on Instagram and similar platforms encourage the display of good times, happy experiences and perfect bodies. This is a topic that has received an enormous amount of attention from campaigners and others concerned about the mental health of young people. How to address the issue is far from clear.

I will make one last point about social media in this chapter, but I will return to the issue when discussing mental health in Chapter 6. Platforms such as TikTok and others act as an echo chamber for risky, unsuitable, sometimes dangerous behaviour. There are, of course, enormous benefits from the use of the digital space. I would not want to overdo the potential negative impact of social media. However, it is important to recognize that support needs to be provided for young people, enabling them to be resilient when they are using social media. I believe this is especially the case for those who are experiencing pruning and other changes to brain structure. They will be undergoing changes in their cognitive skills that may make them vulnerable to the pressures they experience on social media platforms. The understanding we have gained concerning the "social brain" may be helpful in this regard.

THE SOCIAL BRAIN AND COGNITIVE DEVELOPMENT

Many writers have noted that social skills depend on the cognitive maturation that is taking place during these years. Social skills and new ways of thinking go hand-in-hand. What are these new ways of thinking? Firstly, teenagers develop the capacity to think about future possibilities. They are not limited to focussing on the present. Young people become able to switch between the concrete situation (the here and now) and abstract possibilities (the future).

Thinking in abstract terms allows other changes to take place. The individual can see that many situations are not clear-cut – either good or bad. Individuals begin to recognize the grey areas and see that the world is more complex than it was seen to be during childhood. Abstract thinking allows for scientific reasoning. Implicit in any science is the ability to test out hypotheses. If I do this, what will follow? How does one process or experiment differ from another? How can I compare the two?

There are some other important aspects of cognitive maturation that are significant for social skills. One of these is what is called metacognition. This refers to the ability to evaluate one's own thoughts. Did I get that right? Should I have approached it differently? How could I have changed my thinking? It is this skill that underlies the ability to think about other people's thoughts. This is the capacity that underlies self-evaluation.

In terms of the development of social skills, the following features of cognition contribute to this process:

* the recognition of emotion
* perspective-taking
* social evaluation

As the social world of the teenager widens, the skills that allow safe navigation of that world become ever more important. This was always the case when relationships occurred in actual settings. Today, however, many relationships and interactions take place online. In this case, these skills are of even greater importance.

Readers may wish to point out that all these skills are present in childhood. After all, even three and four-year-olds know when Mummy is cross, or when Daddy is sad. Young children are also able to have a sense of someone else's viewpoint, or even to learn that others can comment on their clothes or their mood. This is, of course, true. What is happening, however, is that, as a result of cognitive maturation, these skills are becoming more sophisticated and refined.

EMOTION RECOGNITION

Recognition of emotion in the human face may at first appear to be a very basic skill. However, it is an essential aspect of the ability to stay safe in social situations, manage conflict and respond appropriately when with other people. Knowing when someone is angry by the expression on their face is a good example of such a skill. Being able to do this successfully often determines the outcome of an interaction.

Research has highlighted three key findings concerning the recognition of emotion. The first of these is a specific area in the brain dedicated to facial recognition. This is known as the **fusiform face area**. It is sited in the temporal lobe of the cortex, located at the back of the brain. This area has close links to the visual cortex, also located at the back of the brain. We have learnt that this area plays a vital role in facial recognition, since when it is damaged, the individual has great difficulty in recognizing faces. The fusiform face area can be shown to have links to other areas which play a role in the interpretation of faces. All of these can be shown to mature as the young person gets older and cognitive skills improve.

The second finding is that the recognition of emotion becomes progressively more sophisticated. While some emotions such as happiness or sadness can be recognized by young children (as I have noted), the recognition of more complex emotions only becomes possible during the teenage years. Emotions which show in the face, such as surprise or fear, are harder to interpret. The ability to recognize these emotions only develops gradually as the individual moves into adolescence.

The third finding is that, in young people, the amygdala plays a key role in emotion recognition. A number of studies have shown that, in teenagers, the amygdala is much more engaged in facial recognition than it is in adults. As a result, the young person is more likely to be influenced by her or his emotions when recognizing emotions in others. This, of course, may lead to confusion or error. Some writers have called the amygdala the "agent of change in adolescent neural networks". What does this mean? In essence, it means that the amygdala is playing a greater role in the development of social skills. As a result, these years are a period when emotion recognition may be blown off course by factors beyond visualization and cognition.

PERSPECTIVE-TAKING

Perspective-taking is an important social skill. We cannot form or maintain social relationships without being able to see situations from another person's point of view. Researchers have made the point that perspective-taking is essential for the development of autonomy. Why is that? Autonomy involves the ability to think for oneself and behave independently. This requires an awareness of different beliefs and attitudes, and the skills to choose between them.

This is sometimes known as mentalizing. In other words, when we mentalize, we think about the thoughts of other people. This is also sometimes referred to as having a theory of mind. This means that we have a theory of how other people are thinking. During the course of this chapter, I will show how significant this theory of mind can be for the developing teenager.

In order for us to think about other people's thoughts, at least three areas of the brain are involved. The first is the area related to vision, concerning the detection of stimuli such as the appearance of the face, gestures and other non-verbal cues. The second area has to do with the processing of emotion. As we know, this is the amygdala and associated structures. Thirdly, we have the area that is concerned with memory and reasoning. This last area is the one I have referred to as the prefrontal cortex. This is sometimes known as the "command and control centre" of the brain.

These areas of the brain have to work together. How does this develop? Sometime between the ages of three and five, children begin to understand that other people think and feel differently from their own way of thinking. However, this form of perspective-taking is limited. It might involve understanding the feelings of a friend, or that the room looks different if you see it from another angle. What is known as social perspective-taking takes longer to develop.

Social perspective-taking involves not only being able to ascribe complex emotions to other people, it also involves being able to see things from a third-person perspective. A good example is the recognition that the behaviour of one friend may impact the feelings of another friend, even when one's own feelings are different from both of the others.

SOCIAL EVALUATION

This idea of social perspective-taking links nicely with what is known as social evaluation. This term refers to the process of being evaluated by others, as well as the skill of assessing someone at first meeting. How do you work out if the person is friendly or a threat? This is a skill that enables the individual to stay safe in social situations, especially those that are new or unfamiliar. It is a skill that has become even more important as social situations are navigated in the online as well as the offline worlds.

Two aspects of teenage development come together when we consider social evaluation. In the first place, puberty leads to a changing body. There is a change in the way young people look at themselves, and therefore at the world around them. Not surprisingly, teenagers become acutely aware of their appearance. Research shows that nearly half of all teenage girls feel dissatisfied with their bodies. The figure is lower for boys, but there is still a significant group who worry about how they look.

The second aspect of development that affects social evaluation is linked to cognition. Combined with a changing appearance, there is the ability to think about what others think. This is the mentalizing skill I described earlier. Young people start to think about how others view them. As the body changes, and as identity questions come to the fore, the teenager becomes "preoccupied with the self". A nice way to think about this is to reflect on what has been called "the imaginary audience". The teenager spends time imagining that they are on stage. The whole world is looking, and this can lead to intense self-consciousness.

This self-consciousness very often leads to a stage when the young person becomes so focused on their own world that it becomes difficult to think about others. This has come to be known as "adolescent egocentrism". One father described this to me as follows: "When they get to this stage they go into a long, long tunnel, and all they can see at the end of the tunnel is themselves".

All readers who know teenagers will recognize this stage. A well-known study demonstrated this nicely by placing young people and adults behind a one-way screen. On the other side of the screen was a corridor where people were constantly walking by. The participants know that the onlookers can see them, but they cannot see the onlookers. An area of the brain associated with physical pain was activated in such situations. For this reason, embarrassment has been called "social pain". Interestingly, adults adjusted quickly to this situation, and the activation in their brains calmed down. Not so with teenagers. For this age group, the activation continued for longer, and reached higher levels. In this way, researchers were able to demonstrate how "social pain" was more significant for young people than it was for adults.

We know that acceptance by their peer group plays a big part in the lives of young people. For this reason, social evaluations come to assume a greater degree of significance. The fear of rejection can be crippling for some in this age group. It is not surprising that observation by others has a greater impact on brain function in teenagers than it does in adults.

It is important to recognize that social skills such as these are not usually the focus of attention in the school curriculum. However, they are extremely important, and are underpinned by a range of cognitive skills. Social and cognitive skills usually develop hand-in-hand. There are wide individual differences in the speed and manner in which these skills come to the fore.

The deployment of these skills can be witnessed in the popularity and status of individuals within the peer group. There is no doubt that the more popular individuals will be the ones who have the most advanced social skills. We still know little about how these skills develop. It is probable that this development is partly to do with the growth of cognitive skills, but it is also to do with role models and social learning in the family. Readers should note that being socially skilled is relevant not only within the peer group but also in the wider world. Being socially skilled helps in the classroom, but it also helps in the family and within other social settings.

REJECTION, ISOLATION AND LONELINESS

There are those who go through their teenage years without friends. Some cope well with this situation, either finding support from the family, or getting immersed in an activity or hobby which takes the place of friendship. Of course, this is not always the case. Some experience rejection from their peer group because of their own aggressive or inappropriate behaviour. Others may find themselves isolated because of poor social skills or extreme shyness. A third group may struggle because of bullying. All these situations are painful, both for the young person and for the parents who may have to watch from the sidelines.

All these situations may have an impact on brain development. As I have noted, engagement in the social environment allows for the maturation of the social brain. When this engagement is hindered or interrupted, the processes which build up the social brain are impacted. However, each situation is different, and can lead to different consequences.

Looking first at those who are isolated, some may have had earlier problems with friendship in primary school, while others may find the start of adolescence especially difficult. These challenges may well be linked to delayed puberty and to the associated lag in brain development. Others who experience rejection may try to make friends but find themselves rebuffed. This will be because of behaviour that is irritating or unwelcome. It may also be because of behaviour that does not fit with the social expectations of others. Underlying this, it is likely that some of the features of social brain development that I have mentioned are in some way delayed. The skills underlying emotion recognition, perspective-taking and social evaluation may all be affected, and lead to limitations in the ability to make friendships and fit in with the peer group.

It is important to recognize that social skills can be learned. It is possible, for example, to help an extremely shy teenager become more confident. Giving help with aspects of behaviour such as perspective-taking can lead to a change in attitude, and to increasing self-confidence in social situations. It is also possible to help those who have an aggressive approach to learn to moderate their behaviour when in social situations.

This links to the subject of bullying. An enormous amount has been written about bullying, and this is not the place to go into any depth about the topic. However, all that has been said so far in this chapter can be applied to the question of bullying. In the context of brain development, some deficits of the social brain are likely to be at the heart of bullying. If young people can develop skills in emotion recognition, for example, such skills will lead to a moderation of hurtful behaviour. Social evaluation might also play a part. Being able to recognize how others see you leads to a more mature understanding of one's part in the peer group. Bullying involves a complex set of behaviours, and the social brain will play only one part in the overall picture. Nonetheless, there is much to be gained by looking at bullying from the perspective of the social brain.

CONCLUSION

To conclude, I will give an example of how the brain is engaged when a young person is in a challenging social situation. Imagine a teenage girl hanging around with a group of peers. She thinks she hears someone making a nasty remark about her best friend. What does she do? She has to assess a range of cues from others in the group. What is the emotion on the face of the girl who made the remark? What is the emotion on the faces of others? She then has to decide on a course of action. She weighs up different alternatives.

She has to use her memory of other social situations, and the reactions of others at those times. She then has to predict how others in the group will react, depending on how she behaves. A situation like this involves a huge range of brain functions, all of which have to take place within a few seconds.

Learning how to manage social relationships, how to form friendships, and how to keep oneself safe within a group, are hugely important features of growing up. As I have shown, these skills, as well as many others, are directly linked to the maturation of the brain. All these skills offer positive advantages in relationships with other key figures, both adults and peers. In addition, I have also shown how brain development can lead to short-term deficits. "Preoccupation with the self" and the notion of "the imaginary audience" refer to some of the limitations that occur during this particular stage. It is important for adults who live and work with young people to be aware of both the positives and negatives inherent in the development of social skills during these years.

FURTHER READING

Coleman, J (2021) "*The teacher and the teenage brain*". Routledge. Abingdon, Oxon.

Coleman, J S (1961) "*The adolescent society*". The Free Press. New York.

Crone, E (2017) "The adolescent brain: changes in learning, decision-making and social relations". Psychology Press/Routledge. Abingdon, Oxon.

Downshire, J and Grew, N (2018) "Teenagers translated: a parent's survival guide: 2nd Edition". Vermillion. London.

Jensen, F (2015) "The teenage brain: a neuroscientist's survival guide to raising adolescents and young adults". Harper. New York.

6

WIDE AWAKE AT MIDNIGHT

INTRODUCTION

Many readers will by now be aware that sleep is an important topic where teenagers are concerned. Young people struggle to get to sleep, and are often drowsy in the morning when getting ready for school. Research has shown that the sleep patterns of teenagers differ from those of adults. This finding has been one of the most significant outcomes of the last decade of research into the adolescent brain. In my discussions with young people, many say that they find it hard to get to sleep at night. Of course, this is partly to do with the lure of staying online and checking smartphones at night. In addition, though, we now know that the hormone melatonin is released later in the teenage brain, and therefore plays a big part in affecting sleep in young people.

It is worth noting that not all teenagers experience this problem. Studies show that approximately 25% do not experience sleep difficulties and some appear to go through these years with no problem getting to sleep. Furthermore, there is a wide variation in the timing of the change in sleep patterns. Some find this change happens shortly after puberty, whilst others manage quite well until later in adolescence. Individual differences are important here, as with so many aspects of teenage development.

DOI: 10.4324/9781003331728-6

Our lives are structured so that young people have to fit into the adult daily timetable. The timing of the adult working day means that the sleep needs of teenagers take second place. There have been some attempts to address this problem, and I will discuss these later in the chapter. However, the priority in our daily routines is to fit in with the working lives of adults. It has proved hard to make any shift in this pattern.

We know that teenagers need more sleep than adults. If you place young people in a sleep laboratory, they are likely to sleep for between nine and ten hours. In the real world, however, young people are getting significantly less than this. Surveys differ, but it is clear that many teenagers are getting only six or seven hours of sleep on school nights. Indeed, teachers tell me that pupils at their schools frequently only get between four and five hours sleep at night. This is a serious worry. For various reasons, sleep is especially important for this age group, and so the lack of it has major implications. In this chapter, I will set out some of the key elements of sleep, while also outlining why sleep matters so much for this age group.

TEENAGE SLEEP

Our sleep pattern is governed by what is called the circadian rhythm. This is essentially a 24-hour body clock that is biologically determined. A good example of this is the fluctuation in our body temperature. This goes up and down, dipping at night and returning to a slightly higher level during the day. This rhythm continues no matter what we are doing during the day or at night.

As far as sleep is concerned, melatonin is the hormone that indicates it is time to go to bed. This hormone is released in the brain, sending the signal that we need to sleep. Again, it is the circadian rhythm that governs the release of melatonin. For most adults, this hormone is released in the brain at approximately the same time each night – say, at 10.30 or 11.00. We have now learnt that the circadian rhythm works in a slightly different manner for most teenagers. In this age group, the release of melatonin is delayed. This means that, for teenagers, melatonin is released about an hour and a half to two hours later than for adults. The teenage circadian rhythm has shifted forward. At the time that adults are ready to go to bed, the teenager's body clock is still in the phase of wakefulness.

This fact has profound implications for the life of the teenager. On weekends or during holidays, young people can sleep on in the morning. However, on school days, this is not possible and as a result, it is common for young people to miss out on much-needed sleep. Because of the body clock, and because melatonin is released later at night, it means that there is still some melatonin active on waking in the morning. The result of this is that some students will remain drowsy during the first hour or so of class. It is interesting to note that adults have virtually no melatonin left in their brains when they wake in the morning.

The phenomenon of being drowsy first thing in the morning at school has now been recognized as a specific condition – known as SCT, or sluggish cognitive tempo. Studies show that this condition applies to roughly 50% of students in the first or second lesson in the morning. Once this is acknowledged by schools, there are things that senior managers can do the moderate the timetable. I will have more to say later in the chapter when I discuss interventions to address the sleep problem.

It may be worth mentioning at this point that the melatonin issue has been relevant in research on the impact of the Covid-19 pandemic on young people in the years 2020 and 2021. Studies of the impact of the lockdowns on teenagers have shown that some have actually benefitted from being at home during this period. In a significant group of young people, well-being actually increased during the years when Covid-19 was most prevalent. During this period, students were being home-schooled and therefore there was no pressure early in the morning to wake and get ready to travel to school. As a result, young people were able to get into a better sleep pattern, thus boosting their sense of well-being. Of course, there were other factors that contributed to well-being, but sleep no doubt played a significant part here.

Sleep patterns are affected not only by melatonin but by other elements that need to be taken into account. One of the most important of these is artificial light. Numerous experiments have shown that the presence of electric light can delay the release of melatonin. Thus, a teenager reading in a bedroom with bright lights switched on is likely to experience an even later release of melatonin. In addition, electric light from lamps or from ceiling lights is not the only source of light. We now know that the LED light from smartphones or laptops also influences the release of melatonin. The more a young person is exposed to artificial light, the more they are likely to experience a delay in melatonin release and therefore a delay in becoming sleepy at night.

Many commentators have argued that the reason teenagers find it hard to get to sleep at night has more to do with social media than melatonin. If young people are absorbed by what is happening on their phones, or if they need to be alert to messages or posts, then it is not surprising that they may find it hard to switch off at night. This phenomenon has been named FOMO (fear of missing out). There is no doubt that the pressures and enticements of the online world are hard to resist. Adults have discovered this as well! Nonetheless, there are things that can be done about it. Later in the chapter, I will discuss interventions, including the ways that parents and families can help young people get better sleep. At that point, I will come back to the effects of social media.

WHAT HAPPENS DURING SLEEP?

It is now time to turn to an examination of what actually happens when we are asleep. Many people have the sense that sleep is a time of rest. Having a time at night when we are asleep is a way of refreshing ourselves, so that we are ready for the next day. In some senses, this is correct, but in fact there are times at night when our brains are as active as they are during the day. Much of our knowledge of what actually happens during sleep has only been discovered in the last decade or so.

For the purposes of simplicity, I will distinguish between two phases of sleep. There are in fact at least five phases, but for our purposes two is quite enough! One phase is known as deep sleep, when there are no rapid eye movements (NREM sleep). The second phase is REM sleep. During this phase, rapid eye movements take place, sleep is shallower, and it is likely that it is during this phase that dreaming occurs.

I have already said that sleep is especially important for teenagers. Why should this be so? First, it is during sleep that essential growth hormones are released. The significance of this is obvious. The teenage years are a time of growth and development in all parts of the body. Furthermore, as I have indicated, this is a time of major change in the brain. It is a hugely influential stage of maturation, and so growth hormones are needed more than at other times.

The second finding from recent research is that certain phases of sleep are linked to the process of pruning that I discussed in Chapter 1. Pruning is the process whereby unwanted neurons and connections are allowed to die away, making room for more efficient brain function. Studies have shown that the intensity of deep sleep (NREM sleep) increases in line with the intensity of pruning during the adolescent years. Then, as the brain gradually matures, the pruning dies down, and the proportion of deep sleep during the night also decreases. From this, we can see that the essential movement towards maturation in the brain is closely linked to patterns of sleep for young people.

There is one further process that needs to be highlighted when sleep is being considered. The brain is, of course, highly active during the day. One of the results of this activity is the production of waste material surrounding the neurons. The firing of neurons is both a chemical and an electrical process. As the neurons fire, sending signals around the brain, they create waste products. One necessity for a fully functioning brain is to have these waste products cleared up after a day's activity.

This is the role of some types of glial cells. Some have called these cells helper cells, as they provide support for the brain in various ways. One particular glial cell acts almost like a vacuum cleaner, clearing away and recycling the waste material. The lesson is clear – without sufficient sleep, the glial cells and other structures cannot do their work. We need our brains to be cleaned up every night, otherwise we will not function well the next day.

SLEEP AND LEARNING

It is now time to explore some of the associations between sleep and learning. It has long been known that sleep can enhance memory. Indeed, Greek philosophers wrote about this many centuries ago. However, it was not until the 1950s, when REM and NREM sleep was better understood, that we learnt more about the process of memory consolidation. Studies compared those who had more or less of the two main phases of sleep. The results indicate that it is during deep sleep that memory consolidation takes place.

In recent years, we have learnt more about how this consolidation takes place. By putting electrodes on different parts of the brain during sleep, it is possible to identify the processes taking place at night. In essence, the slow brain waves of deep sleep operate as a postal service. These brain waves send packets of information from the short-term memory store in the hippocampus to the long-term store in the cortex at the front of the brain. It is truly remarkable that we are now able to understand this process. It appears that even a short nap during the day can lead to memory consolidation, as long as there is sufficient deep sleep during this time.

Another way to look at this is to explore how the timing of learning impacts on memory. Many experiments have shown that the later in the day learning takes place, the better the retention on the following day. Here is one good example. One group of learners were asked to memorize a task early in the day. After each training session, the participants showed improvement in their recall. This is known as the practice effect.

When these participants were tested the next morning, there was a slight loss of the material. They had forgotten some aspects of the task. A second group did the same task, but they did the task before they went to bed at night. The differences between the two groups were remarkable. When these participants returned the next night, they did not show any evidence of forgetting. Indeed, they were able to start additional learning straight away.

It is clear that going to sleep immediately after a learning task enhances memory. The reason has to do with the amount of interference taking place during the day. If one learns in the morning, then the amount of information the brain absorbs during the whole day is enormous. This material interferes with the learning process. If one learns at night, the interference is much less. This enables the brain to absorb new material much more readily. This finding is information that should be available to students everywhere.

SLEEP DEPRIVATION

It will be evident that, if students are finding it hard to get to sleep, and having to get up early for school, they will be missing out on the sleep they need. There has been a lot of concern in how this reduction in sleep affects young people. The terms "sleep deprivation" or "sleep deficit" have been used to describe this situation. There is clearly a very wide variation in the amount of sleep any individual will need. However, most experts in this field agree that anything less than between six and seven hours sleep for a teenager should be classified as "sleep deficit". However, reports from teachers and parents seem to indicate that many young people are today sleeping for five hours or even less.

The implications are clear: too little sleep is bound to have an effect on both learning and on mood and emotion. One good example of this problem has to do with the impact on learning. Two groups of teenagers are asked to memorize a task during the day. One group is asked to sleep normally the next night, while the other group has their sleep continually interrupted. The second group experiences sleep deprivation, and the differences are evident in the results. Those who are getting less sleep show poorer memory the next day.

Many studies have attempted to investigate sleep deprivation and its impact on school performance. There are two ways to do this. Loss of sleep can be artificially created by arranging for groups of students to have different amounts of sleep and comparing their performance. The second way to study this is to consider schools that have different start times in the morning. Later start times allow students to get more sleep. This has been possible in the USA, but there are no schools that are able, or willing, to do this in the UK.

Looking at the first method, the results vary. Broadly speaking, however, findings support the conclusion that the greater the sleep loss, the greater the effect on school performance. When school start times are compared, again, the results indicate that the later the start time, the better the academic results. It has to be said that altering start times in the morning has not been popular in the UK, since it affects teachers and parents. Arranging to begin classes later in the morning may be a good thing for young people, but it does not sit well with the timetables of adults!

This leads on to the question of sleep deprivation and student well-being. There are many studies that illustrate the impact that sleep deprivation has on the mood and mental health of teenagers. The most common finding is that the greater the sleep deficit, the more powerful the effect on emotion. The aspect of mental health that appears to be most impacted by limited sleep is depression. Numerous studies in the USA show a link between having less sleep and low mood.

Some studies have compared having less than seven hours of sleep and having less than five hours of sleep. This research illustrates graphically how sleep is linked to mental health. So, if one compares these two groups, the group having less than five hours of sleep are twice as likely to demonstrate poor learning and to have higher levels of mental health problems.

INTERVENTIONS

There are three types of intervention that have tried to address the problem of sleep deprivation. The first has already been mentioned –

this is the idea of having later school start times. The second intervention is one that introduces what are known as "sleep lessons". In the USA, these classes are known as "sleep hygiene lessons". The object here is to inform students about the importance of sleep, and encourage them to find ways of improving their sleep patterns. Lastly, there is work with the whole family. These interventions engage parents and carers with the sleep lessons, and identify strategies that can work in the home.

As I have noted, the option of delayed school start times has not proved popular in the UK. There have been one or two schools that have explored this idea. However, the trials have not lasted long, for the reasons I set out above. Some sixth-form colleges have found this easier to introduce since students are mostly coming into school on their own. However, the notion of later school start times has simply not taken off on this side of the Atlantic.

The situation is different in the USA. Here, there has been significant pressure from paediatricians and other professionals to consider this option. In addition, there are many forums raising awareness of the importance of sleep for young people. In the USA, individual states can legislate on this matter, and this allows greater flexibility. Some states, such as California, have amended school start times in recent years. In most states, it is now expected that schools will not start before 8.30, whereas previously some were starting as early as 7.30 in the morning.

The research evidence does bear out the importance of this. In addition to improved learning and better mental health, other measures have also illustrated the benefits. Since many older students in the USA drive to school, researchers looked at traffic accidents. Interestingly, fewer accidents on the road occur when school start times are delayed. Another example is the re-arrangement of the curriculum. Some schools have arranged the curriculum so that tests and exams are not allowed before 10.00 a.m. When comparisons are made with previous arrangements, it becomes clear that achievements in tests improve significantly if performance is measured later in the morning.

Turning now to the question of sleep lessons, a good example comes from the "Teensleep" study, which was carried out in Oxfordshire schools. The study involved four sessions in class with students across the age range. The focus of the sessions was information about sleep but also assistance in understanding what constitutes a good sleep routine. The results indicated a significant increase in knowledge about sleep, but only a moderate change in actual behaviour.

For readers, it is worth noting that the following strategies are suggested as contributing to better sleep and a greater likelihood of overcoming the melatonin effect:

- Turning off digital devices for a period before sleep.
- If possible, putting smartphones and other devices outside the bedroom.
- Turning lights low.
- Using mood music or other activities to aid relaxation.
- Having a hot drink (without caffeine).
- Most important, getting into a regular bedtime routine.

Of course, for many families, this will not necessarily be easy to introduce. As we have noted, social media creates a strong pull, and this is especially true at night time. However, throughout this chapter, I have been emphasizing the importance of sleep. I will return to the policies and practices that parents can develop to address these issues in the last chapter of the book.

It is interesting to note that a study in Australia illustrated well the role that parents can play here. In this study, the researchers compared sleep lessons for students alone, and sleep lessons when parents were also present. The results were clear. When students attended on their own, they gained knowledge, but there was little change in behaviour. This was the same finding as was published in the study from Oxford. However, when these sleep lessons were offered to both students and parents together, the results were different. In this condition, there was an impact on sleep behaviour. Students in this case were able to increase their actual hours of sleep following the intervention.

To sum up, as there is an increasing awareness of the role that sleep plays in our well-being and in intellectual performance, I believe this will become a topic of greater importance in the future. It is clear that finding ways to allow or encourage young people to get more sleep does have an impact on their lives. Nothing could be more important than that.

CONCLUSION

I will conclude this chapter by considering why it is that teenage sleep patterns should be different from those of adults. Why is that melatonin is released later at night in the teenage brain? It is certainly a puzzle, and one that surely has an explanation. But what explanation is there? I have found two possible suggestions that have been put forward. Neither is entirely satisfactory. Readers can make up their own minds, and, of course, discuss this with their teenage sons and daughters.

One explanation is rooted in evolutionary theory. In this theory, it is proposed that many thousands of years ago when humans were still nomadic, it was essential for a watch to be kept at night in case of predators or warring tribes. The role of keeping watch at night was given to the younger members of the tribe who were just reaching adulthood. The longer they could stay awake, the better for the tribe. Thus, melatonin release gradually altered to help those keeping watch to avoid sleep for longer into the night.

A second explanation has to do with the social circumstances of adolescent development. For young people to grow into independence they need time apart from their parents. If they can stay awake later at night, then time becomes available for them to pursue their own activities. At this point, they are no longer being monitored by the adults in the family. If this is the case, then the later release of melatonin allows the young person to stay awake when parents are asleep.

Both these explanations have been put forward by experts on the science of sleep. In both cases, we can see how the brain and the environment interact. Irrespective of which explanation has the greater merit, the later release of melatonin is being affected by social and environmental factors. Throughout the book, I have emphasized the fact that brain development during the teenage years does not occur in isolation from the circumstances surrounding the individual. Brain development is driven by a range of biological and genetic factors. Yet these factors cannot be the only ones that impact on the brain. The study of sleep is a nice illustration of this conclusion.

FURTHER READING

Coleman, J (2021) "*The teacher and the teenage brain*". Routledge. Abingdon, Oxon.

Foster, R (2022) "*Life time: the new science of the body clock and how it can revolutionize your sleep and health*". Penguin Life. London.

Walker, M (2018) "*Why we sleep: the new science of sleep and dreams*". Allen Lane/Penguin. London.

7

IS THIS THE "SNOWFLAKE GENERATION"?

INTRODUCTION

There is no topic more important to consider than the mental health of our children and young people. This is a topic that has been high on the agenda for some time now, and there are many questions that arise when we address this. What is the difference between mental health and mental illness? What links can be made between brain development and mental well-being? And then there is the question that is implied in the title of the chapter – is this generation really more vulnerable? Has mental ill-health in teen-agers worsened in recent years? And if this is the case, what is the reason for this change?

All these are challenging questions, and I will cover them all in this chapter. I worry about using the term "snowflake generation" as it may imply an underlying weakness or frailty in young people today. It is a phrase that is often used, not only in the media, but by profes-sionals as well. If it is legitimate, then we need to think about how we can address it. If it does not stand up to examination, then we need to find ways of rebutting it. The title of the chapter is a way of indicating that it is a question for debate.

DOI: 10.4324/9781003331728-7

MENTAL HEALTH OR MENTAL ILL-HEALTH

One of the problems that has plagued the field of mental health is the difficulty of terminology. It would seem sensible to look at this in terms of a continuum, with good mental health at one end, and poor mental health on the other. In this sense, we could think of illness at one end and well-being as being at the positive end of the spectrum. Unfortunately, however, the term mental health is too often used in the negative sense, referring to disorder or illness.

In recent years, there has been an increased focus on the positive end of the spectrum, which can only be a good thing. Nonetheless, the terminology here is also problematic, since terms such as happiness, well-being, emotional intelligence and resilience are all used by different authors to refer to something broadly similar. Then there is the question of how to define mental ill-health where teenagers are concerned. One of the frequent queries that concerns parents is how to distinguish between the expected ups and downs of adolescence, and something more serious that requires professional help.

It is usually considered that the following signs are a useful guide that something is more than a transient phase of development:

- The problem is persistent, lasting more than a couple of weeks.
- There is a sense of hopelessness and continuing low mood.
- The young person regularly expresses negative, distressing or unusual thoughts.
- Physical symptoms, such as eating or sleep problems, are also present.
- There are significant changes in activities, such as going to school or being with friends, that were previously unremarkable.

In this chapter, I will use the phrase mental ill-health or disorder when referring to the negative end of the spectrum. The majority of our discussion here will apply to this subject. This is not the place to discuss well-being – the positive end of the spectrum – in any depth. I will first look at the question of stress, and how this is linked with brain function in young people. I will then go on to consider whether there are features of the changing brain that may contribute to mental ill-health. Following this, I will explore the question of whether early trauma affects brain development, and I will also look at conditions that are usually considered to be included in what is known as neuro-diversity. I will conclude the chapter by returning to the phrase I have used in its title, and ask whether this is a legitimate way to describe the current generation of young people.

STRESS AND THE BRAIN

Much of what we know about the present generation of teenagers tells us that many experience life as stressful. When interviewed, young people frequently talk about the pressures that come from school, as well as concerns about family and about friendships. Of course, in recent years, the pandemic of 2020 and 2021 has also led to sig-nificant challenges for this age group. Not all have been negatively impacted, but even as I write this in 2023, there are ongoing prob-lems for some groups which are a result of the Covid-19 lockdowns.

As I pointed out in Chapter 3, stress affects the amygdala and other areas of the brain to do with the processing of emotion. The teenage amygdala has less capacity to deal with fear or anger, thus leading to more extreme responses to these emotions. The emotions of worry, anxiety and other similar feelings are associated with levels of cortisol in the brain. Research has shown that cortisol levels are somewhat higher in adolescence than in adulthood.

This finding leads to the conclusion that young people are likely to find things like decision-making more difficult in situations of high emotion. Looking at brain function in these circumstances, it would appear that self-control and thinking about consequences involves more regions of the brain. The more demanding the task, the greater the individual depends on brain connectivity. In adults, this connectivity is still present, even under stressful circumstances. In teenagers, however, it appears that such connectivity deteriorates in stressful or emotional situations. The older the individual, the more advanced the capacity of the brain to utilize the prefrontal cortex and therefore to manage stress. To put it another way, in young people, the circuits between the prefrontal cortex and the amygdala are not yet fully mature.

Another topic to consider under this heading is the relationship between stress and learning. We know that learning is best when stress is at a moderate level. This creates motivation to learn. Low levels of stress are associated with low motivation. The key issue is that high levels of stress cause anxiety, and that interferes with the learning process. As far as brain function is concerned, the hippocampus plays a part here.

Readers will remember from Chapter 1 that the hippocampus is sited next to the amygdala, and thus is easily affected by emotion. When stressed, the individual will be experiencing heightened activity in the amygdala. This in turn affects the memory processing that is taking place in the hippocampus. The ability to learn is thus reduced because of the close connection between the two sites. Some studies show that the amygdala becomes enlarged because of stressful experiences. This then means that it is more difficult for the controlling effects of the prefrontal cortex to operate and calm things down.

In Chapter 4, I discussed the notion of executive function. The four elements associated with this are working memory, inhibition, resistance to interference and flexibility. Recent research has shown how stress can inhibit executive function as a result of the release of stress hormones such as cortisol. These substances prepare the individual to respond to threat. As I have noted, oxygen is directed to the muscles and in the visual cortex, the eyes become focused on possible danger, and so on. In dealing with threat, the brain directs resources away from the areas to do with executive function such as working memory. It is in this way that stress reduces the capacity to learn.

THE BRAIN AND MENTAL ILL-HEALTH

The first point to note is the interaction between brain development and the environment. I have emphasized this throughout the book.

Everything we know illustrates how the changes in the brain during the teenage years are impacted by what is happening around the individual. Thus, both factors need to be taken into account. For many years, we have known that enriched environments lead to healthy brain development. We have also been able to see that impoverished environments restrict the development of the brain. Early work on this topic was done on mice and other animals. In recent years, there have been studies of children and young people growing up in poverty. These show the same results. The greater the poverty and deprivation, the slower the brain development during the teenage years.

When we consider the role of the brain in mental ill-health, we have to take into account other factors, too. These include the environment in its broadest sense, including the family, the school and the wider neighbourhood. Developmental factors also need to be considered. The young person does not arrive at the age of 11 without going through childhood. Thus, what happened in those early years has an influence on their teenage years. Timing matters, too. If stressful events all happen at the same time, this is likely to have a greater impact than if the stresses occur over a period of years.

Turning now to the brain, what can we say about the impact of neurological changes in the causation of mental ill-health? You will remember that, in the brain, electrical impulses travel from one neuron to the next along nerve fibres. In order to do so they jump across the synapses, the little gaps along the nerve fibre. Within the synapse there are neurotransmitters, sometimes called chemical messengers. These are of two types – those that facilitate the transmission of the message, and those that inhibit it or shut it down. In essence, this is an on/off mechanism.

I discussed this process in Chapter 1. The brain is like a railway network, with a signalling system which prevents the system from breaking down. There are literally millions, perhaps billions, of messages travelling around the brain at any one moment. If, for one reason or another, the on/off process is not acting effectively, the individual will be bombarded with impulses. Thus, it will be difficult to sort out which should be attended to, and which should be ignored.

Any failure of the inhibitory mechanisms in the brain may lead to various problems associated with mental ill-health. Difficulties with attention, or a greater likelihood of impulsive behaviour, can all be explained by poor functioning of the signalling system. A classic example of this is attention deficit hyperactivity disorder (ADHD). Here, the young person struggles with being able to pay attention in class or with keeping still for any length of time. It will be evident that, if the inhibitory mechanism does not function properly, then problems, such as poor concentration or constant fidgeting, will be the result.

Mood disorder may also be linked to various features of brain function. In Chapter 3, I discussed the variation in hormone levels that occurs during brain development in the teenage years. While it is important to note that there are different types of depression, some forms of mood disorder may be affected by the hormone balance in the brain. One type of depression arises because of external events, such as trauma or loss. However, another type of depression occurs without any obvious external cause. It is this type of depression that may be linked to hormonal levels. Thus, for example, if levels of serotonin are too low, this may have an impact on mood. This can have the effect of making the young person feel very sad, hopeless or disengaged.

Anxiety may also be affected by hormone levels. There are numerous hormones that have an impact on anxiety levels in the brain. I have noted cortisol, but there are also hormones such as GABA and others that play a role here. GABA is instrumental in reducing the excitability of neurons, and thus helping to control anxiety or fear. When GABA is too low, it may be more difficult to control unhelpful emotions. This provides another example of the way in which what is happening in the brain may be linked to mental ill-health.

The last point to make here has to do with the degree of change that is happening during the teenage years. As a result of pruning and of maturation, the brain undergoes a major change during these years. As with all developmental processes, some individuals will manage change without too much distress or difficulty. However, there are some who will inevitably find this process a challenging one.

The restructuring of the brain that takes place in adolescence is hugely significant. As I have said, this is the biggest change in the brain at any time apart from in the first three years of life. This stage is sometimes known as a "sensitive period". What matters during these years matters very much for later development. The very fact that it is such a critical moment in brain development will affect individuals in different ways. Some will cope well, whilst others will find the restructuring and re-organization of the brain difficult to manage. It is these individuals who may be especially vulnerable during this period of their lives.

NEURODIVERSITY

This term has come to apply to both ADHD and to autism. I have dealt briefly with ADHD in the previous section, so here I will concentrate on autism. There are different terms that are used to describe autism. For some time, this was known as ASD, or autistic spectrum disorder. It has now been recognized that it is incorrect to think about autism as a disorder. Rather, it is better seen as a condition in which the brain works differently from the way brains work in others. It is for this reason that the term neurodiversity, or ASC (autistic spectrum condition), has become more acceptable. Autism is a condition in which the brain is wired in a different way, but it is not necessarily disordered.

It is important to recognize that when we talk of ASC we may be speaking of a very wide range of conditions. Those with this condition can range from having no functional language and severe developmental delay to those who have at least average intelligence and no language delay. What those with ASC have in common includes social communication difficulties, difficulties with cognitive empathy, and difficulties adjusting to unexpected change. However, autism is also associated with cognitive strengths, such as excellent attention to detail, an excellent memory for certain things, and an ability to synthesize or detect patterns. It should also be acknowledged that some with autism have remarkable talents, such as being artistic, or having unusual mathematical ability.

As far as brain development is concerned, it is clear that the brains of those with ASC do function differently from those in the wider population. However, in spite of numerous studies on this topic, there is little evidence that those with ASC have an actual brain disorder. What we have learnt is that there are differences that can be identified in the brains of those with ASC. These include, in some, having a somewhat larger amygdala in childhood, and having some sections of the bridge between the two hemispheres being a bit smaller than in others.

Studies using brain imaging also show differences. On some tasks, those with ASC show less brain activity than other young people. On the other hand, they show greater activity on different tasks, often tasks needing extra vigilance. These differences reflect some of the well-known behavioural markers of ASC, such as extra sensitivity to certain stimuli or greater attention to detail.

There is clearly a wide diversity in the way our brains work. Looking at those with ASC, we can see that their brains process details differently, and pay attention to different cues in social situations. However, there is no evidence that this is an illness. It reflects difference, rather than disorder. It is for this reason that neurodiversity is the preferred term today.

CHILDHOOD TRAUMA

One of the most common questions I am asked following workshops that I deliver on the teenage brain has to do with childhood trauma and its effects. Understandably, those who work with young people who have experienced abuse or other traumatic events during their childhood want to know what effect these experiences will have in the teenage years. In particular, they want to know whether trauma will continue to affect brain development. It is also important to understand whether it is possible for teenagers to recover from earlier traumatic experiences.

These are not easy questions to answer. There is such a wide variety of traumatic events that can impact on a child's life that it is hard to construct studies that provide conclusive answers. Nonetheless, many investigators have been studying this topic over the past decade. The broad conclusion is that there are significant differences in brain function in those who have been exposed to childhood trauma.

The evidence relates to four topics. The topics include the way the individual's brain responds to threatening stimuli, the way the brain processes rewards, the operation of emotion regulation, and, finally, the use of executive function. Almost all studies in this area illustrate that, in these domains, individuals who have been exposed to these early childhood events do show differences in neural functioning. To take one example, where reactions to threat are concerned, there is evidence of both heightened vigilance as well as avoidance. These reactions must reflect ways of coping which were established at earlier times when experiencing unpleasant or frightening events.

It appears that this pattern of brain activity is adaptive in situations of threat. However, such reactions are clearly not helpful as the individual moves away from harmful circumstances and is able to experience more nurturing and supportive relationships.

It should be noted that there are many challenges in carrying out this type of research. It is hard to find matched samples or populations of children in order to draw comparisons between those who have experienced trauma and those who have not. Also, there are many different types of adverse experience that might be said to be traumatic. Lastly, many children who have experienced these adverse circumstances have histories of multiple placements and disrupted lives, so that studying these groups poses particular problems.

Thinking about this leads us on to thinking about the broader question of whether early trauma has a long-lasting impact on brain development. Do the indicators that I have mentioned above, such as the change in response to threat, have a continuing impact on the individual? The simple answer to this is that we still do not know. However, there are some clues. First, it is the case that the human brain is amazingly plastic. This means that it has the capacity to repair itself. There are numerous examples of how, even after injury, the brain adapts and returns to normal functioning. There is also some useful information on this question from studies of adoption and fostering.

These studies show that the earlier the child is removed from the harmful environment, the more likely it is that the outcome will be a positive one. In addition, studies of resilience indicate that much will depend on the type of environment into which the child moves following abuse or trauma. The more supportive the environment, the more likely it is that the individual will overcome earlier adversity.

There is much that we still do not know about childhood trauma and its effect on the brain. Nonetheless, there are some positive indications. The brain has a remarkable capacity to adjust and adapt. The more the world around the child or young person can provide nurture and support, the greater the chance of being able to overcome earlier adversity.

SOCIAL MEDIA

As I have mentioned in earlier chapters, the role of social media in the lives of young people is hugely significant. Here, I want to look briefly at this topic in the context of understanding brain development and mental ill-health. The question that worries adults has to do with the possibility that information on social media leads to harmful behaviour. How likely is it that accessing posts, images and information on websites will lead to actual suicide, self-harm or an eating disorder?

This is a vexed question, and one that has no simple answer. In years gone by, anxiety focused on violence in films and video games. Huge sums were spent on research to try and establish whether seeing violence on screen led to violent behaviour. The findings led to the conclusion that perhaps, sometimes, this may happen. But only if the individual already has a propensity to be violent anyway. Today we are concerned with the same riddle, except that now we are asking the question about mental health.

Most researchers have concluded that it is unlikely that an individual would be motivated to harm themselves simply as a result of seeing images or posts on screen. What is most likely to happen, scientists have concluded, is that self-harm is already occurring when the individual starts exploring the online world concerning this type of behaviour.

In the literature, there are numerous examples of young people using the online world to learn more about behaviour they are already engaging in. They may be looking to gather support from others who are experiencing similar mental health problems, or seeking therapy of one sort or another for their troubles. The model that sees this as an indicator of "contagion" is not supported by the evidence. Thus, it is unlikely that someone can catch a certain type of behaviour by seeing it demonstrated on screen.

It has also been reported that many young people say they turn to the online world following conflict with their parents or other key adults. In some cases, teenagers disclose their self-harming behaviour to the adults close to them, only to be met by anger, disapproval or disbelief. Under such circumstances, when young people are in distress and feel rejected by adults, they turn to the internet for an alternative source of information and assistance.

One other issue should be noted here. How does screen time affect brain development? In the early years of social media use, when the amount of screen time was an issue for adults, there were some who put forward the idea that too much time online "rots the brain". I think we now know that this is a simplistic view. Of course, too much time spent looking at a screen will not be good for anyone. However, the question has now turned into a focus on what the child or young person is doing on the internet, rather than how many hours are spent in front of a screen.

This question concerning the link between screen time and mental health has been the focus of numerous research studies. Whilst anxiety among adults concerned for their children's welfare remains, studies show a more nuanced picture. Firstly, the pandemic of 2020/2021 has meant that adults themselves are spending more time online. This has led to a recognition that concern about screen time should apply to all, not just to the younger generation.

Secondly, studies of mental health and screen time for young people do not spell doom and gloom. Of course, it does depend on the amount of time spent online. Sitting up for hours at night gaming is clearly going to have a negative impact on all aspects of development. However, most studies show that, as long as the use of the internet is kept within reasonable bounds, time spent online can have a positive effect on cognitive development and on behaviour. There is little evidence to show that using the internet has an impact on brain development, so long, as I say, as screen time is not excessive.

"THE SNOWFLAKE GENERATION?"

It is time now to turn to the question posed at the beginning of the chapter. Is the term "snowflake generation" a legitimate description of young people today? As with many questions posed in this chapter, it is far from easy to provide a simple answer. Turning first to the evidence on mental ill-health, there are big challenges in obtaining reliable and up-to-date data. We need high-quality research, using the same methods, over a period of time, in order to obtain reliable answers.

The UK government carried out major studies of mental ill-health in children and young people in 1999 and 2004. There was then a gap until, in 2017, another major study took place. As will be obvious, the timing of these studies is far from ideal. However, as a result of the pandemic in 2020/2021, further research has been carried out, although none has been as thorough as the 2017 study.

Looking at the data from the 2017 study, approximately 14% of young people between the ages of 11 and 16 had a mental health condition. In the younger group, there was little difference between boys and girls, but this altered in the older group, where girls showed higher levels of disorder. Broadly, behaviour problems were more common in boys, whilst emotional problems such as anxiety and depression were more common in girls.

If we look at change over time, there has been some increase in mental ill-health since 1999, although this change – from 11% to 14% – is hardly dramatic. Unfortunately, figures are not available for the group aged between 17 and 19, since these data were not collected in 1999 and 2004. It is very difficult to assess what lies behind the increase in disorders. It may be that there has been better reporting, or that there was more awareness of mental health issues over this time period.

Another possible explanation is that mental health services have been reduced over this time period. Due to the period of "austerity" following the change of government in 2010, many services were restricted or discontinued. More limited access to services will inevitably lead to more distress. Longer waiting times for appointments, combined with reduced staffing, will be bound to affect levels of mental ill-health amongst all age groups, but especially among children and young people.

During the pandemic of 2020/2021, there were many research groups trying to look at whether the mental health of children and young people was impacted by the experience of lockdown and home learning. Only in 2023 were we able to obtain an overview of the picture created by Covid-19. In summary, there does not appear to have been an overall increase in mental ill-health among children and young people. However, the results of the research show that certain groups were more affected than others.

Those with special educational needs, those with pre-existing conditions, and those living in poverty or deprivation, all showed increased levels of distress and mental ill-health. Among teenagers, it appeared to be the older age groups who showed higher levels of mental ill-health. As far as the types of conditions are concerned, it was eating disorders that showed the greatest increase among young people. Against expectations, self-harm and suicide did not show any significant increase in this period.

How does all this relate to the possible increased frailty of the present generation of young people? As will be obvious, it is very difficult to compare generations, since the methods to do this are simply not available. However, there are some pointers that we can use for this purpose. The research evidence, such as it is, does not appear to support a marked increase in mental ill-health. However, awareness of mental health and mental illness has increased dramatically. There is much more focus on well-being and good mental health in schools, and this reflects a change in attitudes in society generally. In addition, most secondary schools now include some elements of mental health education in their Personal, Social and Health (PSHE) programmes.

Added to this, services have been cut, as I have noted above. If governments reduce services for mental ill-health, it follows that problems will increase. It should also be noted that stress in the school system in the UK has increased as well. Inspections by OFSTED, and the pressure on schools to show high levels of exam success, all impact on students. There are many reports of young people agreeing that they experience high levels of stress as a result of their school experience.

All in all, I believe that there is simply no evidence to support the notion of a "snowflake" generation. Quite the contrary. If we consider the pressures and the circumstances that face this generation as they grow into adulthood, we should be conscious of the challenges they are facing. As well as being a period of rapid change in the brain, it is also an age when society offers little to support this generation. I would argue that it is more likely to be a greater awareness of mental health and mental illness rather than any change in young people themselves that lies behind any notion of frailty or vulnerability.

CONCLUSION

In this chapter, I have considered a wide range of issues relating to mental health and the brain. I have questioned the concept of "the snowflake generation" and come to the view that there is little empirical evidence to support this. Yes, the incidence of mental health problems has increased, but there are many different reasons for this. In this chapter, I have also looked at conditions such as ADHD and neurodiversity, and explored how these conditions link with what is happening in the brain. Other key issues that have been included are stress in adolescence, the role of social media, and the question of whether trauma in childhood has a long-term impact on the changes that take place in the brain during the teenage years. It is clear that the brain and the environment interact, so that each influences the other. Enriching environments enhance brain development, but restrictive environments have the capacity to slow down brain development during critical periods. Nonetheless, the brain is inherently plastic, so it has the capacity to recover from negative events. This is a hopeful message. Where environments provide support and nurture, teenagers have opportunities to grow and thrive.

FURTHER READING

Barrett, L F (2020) *"Seven and a half lessons about the brain"*. Picador. London.

Frydenberg, E (2019) *"Adolescent coping: promoting resilience and well-being: 3rd Edition"*. Routledge. Abingdon, Oxon.

Galvan, A (2017) *"The neuroscience of adolescence"*. Cambridge University Press. Cambridge.

Jensen, F (2015) *"The teenage brain: a neuroscientist's survival guide to raising adolescents and young adults"*. Harper. New York.

Ogden, T and Hagen, K (2019) *"Adolescent mental health: prevention and intervention: 2nd Edition"*. Routledge. Abingdon, Oxon.

Scott, S (2022) *"The Brain: 10 things you should know"*. Orion Publishing. London.

8

THE TEENAGE BRAIN FOR KEY ADULTS

INTRODUCTION

I started this book by stating that I was going to write about all the usual things to do with teenagers, but just from a different perspective. This perspective is one that takes the brain as its starting point. Throughout this book, I have suggested that, by knowing what is happening in the brain, we, as adults, can take a very different approach to young people. We can show more empathy, and we will have a better understanding of all the aspects of teenage behaviour that are sometimes hard to comprehend.

I want to introduce this last chapter by telling you about the workshops I and other colleagues have been running on the teen brain. At the beginning of each workshop, after introductions and other housekeeping, we usually start with a short activity.

In this activity, we ask the participants to write down four words to describe typical teenage behaviour. They are asked not to think too deeply about this, but to jot down the first words that come into their minds. As you can imagine, most people have little difficulty in completing this task. You can try it yourself if you wish.

There are two striking things about this exercise. In the first place, the great majority of words chosen by those attending the workshops tend to focus on the negative. Very few words feature positive aspects of teenage behaviour, such as: sense of humour, determined, idealistic or good company. The great majority, as I say, are negative.

The second thing about this activity is that almost all the words that people choose can be linked directly to our understanding of the brain. Let me give some examples:

- moody
- angry
- inconsistent
- easily defeated
- sleepy
- only interested in themselves
- contradictory
- very stressed
- argumentative

This is what makes the workshops so fascinating, and useful for those attending. Once participants see the links between the brain and the puzzling behaviours of young people, it is like a "light-bulb moment". This activity provides an excellent introduction to the workshops, and allows us to explore the impact that teenagers have on the key adults around them. We can discuss why it is that so many of the words chosen reflect negative traits, and we can illustrate just why it is useful to learn more about the teenage brain. If you want to know more about these workshops, you can get more information from my website (www.jcoleman.co.uk), and from my book *The Teacher and the Teenage Brain"* (Routledge, 2021).

In this final chapter, I will say something about being a parent of a teenager. I will also discuss the challenges faced by teachers and others in their daily work with young people. I will conclude with a note on the healthy brain and how adults and young people can have an impact on the way their brains develop during adolescence.

BEING A PARENT OF A TEENAGER

Being a parent of a teenager is hard! A mother once said to me: "Being a parent of a teenager is hard, it is harder than being a brain surgeon!" Why should this be so? In the first place, being a parent of a teenager is not the same as being the parent of a younger child. Parents of teenagers are likely to be more isolated than other parents. They do not gather at the school gates. They receive less support than other parents, mainly because there is no acceptable setting where they can get together. Related to this is the fact that this group of parents is more difficult to access, apart from through the school information network. Because there is no obvious gathering place, there is no simple way to provide informal opportunities for advice and support.

In the second place, parents of teenagers are likely to be at a different stage of life. They will be older, more likely to face health or employment challenges, and more likely to have responsibilities for their own parents as well as their teenagers. Their own relationships with partners may be under strain. The optimism and closeness of early marriage may give way to a less satisfying family life. In addition to all this, they may find that, just when they expect to be free of the financial burdens of looking after teenagers, their young people continue to live at home and expect further financial support.

All these factors are associated with the nature of the teenage years. The parenting of young people does carry with it particular challenges. In many respects, it is harder than the parenting of younger children. What exactly is the role of a parent at this time? Many parents I talk to say they do not really understand their role. The teenager is pushing them away. The girl or boy much prefers talking to their friends rather than to the adults in the family. So, what is the point of parents at this stage?

Everything we know tells us that parents of teenagers are just as important as parents of younger children, they are just important in a different way. All the studies show that teenagers do best when their parents remain involved and supportive, even if that is hard at times. One particular problem that parents at this stage face is that parenting practices have to change to reflect the changing needs of the young person. Structures and sanctions for a 14-year-old are not the same as those for an 8-year-old. Making that shift is not always easy, but it is, of course, essential in order to keep up with the needs of young people.

Another factor is that teenagers are adept at finding ways to challenge, infuriate and distress their parents. This is all part of the process of separating and finding a new identity. This is especially difficult for adults, and as a result they may feel ashamed and guilty that they are not able to provide "good parenting". One parent came to a workshop stating: "I am here because I am a crap parent". This is a familiar refrain. Teenagers are skilled at making their parents feel like "crap".

One of the major reasons why it is valuable to learn how the brain develops during these years is that, once parents understand what is happening to their teenager, they will no longer feel worthless and without a role. To help parents understand this, and to make sense of this stage in their child's life, I have developed an explanatory framework. I have called this the STAGE framework, and it goes like this.

THE STAGE FRAMEWORK

This framework is called STAGE because this is a stage in the life course. I believe it is important for parents to recognize that it is a stage, and that things will not stay the same. The young person is going through a process of changing from child to adult, and this means that change will be happening all the time, even if that change is not always visible. The brain is a perfect example of invisible change. I also called the framework STAGE because each of the letters represents a key element of parenting.

THE S STANDS FOR SIGNIFICANCE

The key message here is that the parent matters. Although the teenager is sending the opposite message, without your support and concern, they will be lost. Just like the rest of us, teenagers need love. They need to be valued, and they need to know that they matter to their parents. If your teenager is pushing you away, telling you that you don't understand, don't let that put you off. Stay in there. Parents are the most significant people, and your teenager needs you.

T STANDS FOR TWO-WAY COMMUNICATION

The T in STAGE stands for two-way communication. It is essential to recognize that communication involves both talking and listening. The two things go hand-in-hand. If you are willing to listen, the teenager will be more likely to talk. The teenager's behaviour will have an effect on you. But it works the other way around. The way you behave influences the teenager. Communication between you and your teenager is not just talking, or you asking questions. It is not always easy to get a conversation going. It is not the same as talking to a friend. Be willing to stand back and take your cue from the young person. Most important, try not to interrogate, or nag. The more you show you can listen, the more they will talk.

THE A STANDS FOR AUTHORITY

The way you exercise your authority is central to everything in your relationship with your teenager. There are many different ways in which you can use your power with your son or daughter. You can be more or less demanding in what you expect from the teenager, and in the boundaries and limits that you set. The best option is for the parent to be loving and caring, while at the same time being firm in setting appropriate boundaries. It is best if the parent can also promote autonomy where possible, as long as it is age appropriate and you identify clear goals and expectations.

THE G STANDS FOR GENERATION GAP

What does generation gap mean in this context? Here I am referring to the idea that you may judge your teenager based on your own experiences, rather than on what is happening to them right now. It is hardly a secret that growing up today is utterly different from how it was 30 or 40 years ago. Taking this on board will make communication with your teenager that much easier.

It is not always easy to respect your teenager's views, especially if they conflict with your own values and beliefs. This is one of the reasons why the two generations do not always see eye to eye. Disagreement is not a disaster. You can still have a good relationship, though you may not always have the same ideas about things. Try not to judge your son or daughter because they grow up in a different age from your own. The more you can be open to another point of view, the better your relationship with your teenager will be.

THE E STANDS FOR EMOTION

Parents experience many different emotions in their relationships with their teenagers. There may be anger, sadness, upset, worry, even fury and frustration. All these emotions, and many more, are part of being a parent of a teenager. It is essential to recognize that your son or daughter will also be experiencing a range of emotions, many of them new and confusing. I have talked about this during the course of the book. At times, both parents and young people may be struggling with difficult feelings. By recognizing your feelings, you will have a better chance of managing them.

Try to remember that, whatever your young person is doing or saying, they are not doing it to you, or at you. The feelings they are experiencing are to do with what is happening inside them, and not about what they feel towards you. Learn to take a step back. It can really help to walk away until you have both calmed down. Try to get in touch with how you felt at the same age. As a teenager, you will have struggled with strong and sometimes upsetting feelings, and no doubt you will have had a few difficult times with your own parents. It can help to remember those times.

PARENTING AND THE BRAIN

You may ask how the STAGE framework relates to our understanding of the teenage brain. At the beginning of this chapter, I gave some examples of the words used by parents and other adults to describe typical teenage behaviour. I pointed out that most of the words have direct links to brain development. Examples include references to moods and feelings, sleep, uncertainty and confusion, being self-centred, anxious or stressed, and so on. All these topics have been covered in this book. Once parents realize that the behaviours they find hard to understand can be linked directly to what is happening in the brain, they feel quite differently about their teenager.

This realization makes it so much easier to feel sympathy. It also makes it possible to think about communication in a different light. Greater recognition of what might be happening to the young person brings greater empathy. As many parents say: "I will talk to my son/daughter in a different way now". The insights that come with a knowledge of brain development make it possible to have a shift in relationships, so that the parent can respond in a different manner. I am confident that learning about the brain will lead to parents being able to offer more support and understanding to their teenage sons and daughters.

TEACHERS AND OTHER ADULTS

I have set out why this knowledge can make a difference to the way parents and young people relate to each other. But what about other adults? Is this relevant for them, too? In the workshops that I and others run for teachers, social workers and other professionals, we use the same activity to start things off at the beginning of the event. We ask for four examples of typical teenage behaviour, and we find the same pattern of responses.

On the one hand, these responses refer primarily to negative aspects of behaviour, and on the other, almost all words used can be linked to information about the teenage brain. As with parents, this is useful, as the activity provides a perfect opening and rationale for attendance at the event. Of course, teachers and other adults have somewhat different concerns from those of parents, and we construct the workshops so that these concerns are addressed.

One of the fascinating things about the development of this work has to do with the relevance of this new knowledge to each different profession. There has been some scepticism about whether neuroscience has any place in the training of teachers and the continuing professional development of those already working in schools. A colleague of mine, with tongue in cheek, wrote a paper entitled *From Brain Scan to Lesson Plan* (Paul Howard Jones, 2011. *The Psychologist*. Pages 210–213). The title is intriguing, but as the author knows, it is not possible to go directly from brain imaging to planning a lesson for the classroom. To my mind, there are different issues involved here.

When I have asked teachers what they would like to know about brain development, it is quite clear that they want to know more about the psychology of teenagers. They ask questions about moods and feelings, about understanding consequences, about drowsiness in the classroom, and about differing rates of maturation. This makes it clear to me that what is missing for most teachers in secondary education is a knowledge of adolescent development. The workshops on the brain have the potential to fill an important gap.

Another element of this is what teachers take away from this learning. Here are some typical comments from teachers following workshops on the teenage brain:

- "It has enabled me to explain to students how their brains develop, and why that matters for them."
- "It has made me stop and think, and re-word what I say to the young people I work with."
- "I use it to help teenagers understand that they are not alone, and that it is happening to everyone."
- "It has helped me understand some of the behaviours of my pupils, and so I have adjusted my teaching practice accordingly."

As will be apparent, responses like these make it evident that workshops for teachers can make a significant difference to their responses to their students. As I have noted, these workshops have also been run for other professions, such as social workers, counsellors and others.

Here, again, we can demonstrate the relevance of this knowledge to working with young people. Participants in these workshops from all different professions make similar points.

They note that their colleagues want to learn more about adolescence, and that knowing about the brain fills an important gap. I have been struck by some of the responses, and insights that they gain. One example is a recognition that there is capacity for change. Learning about the rapid change that occurs in the brain, as well as that this is a critical period, leads to an awareness of the opportunities that are offered here if the environment provides the right support.

Another example of the impact of the workshops is a greater sympathy and understanding for emotional meltdowns. As a professional, these are hard to deal with, but knowing about the brain does help adults manage such situations. I remember one social worker saying to me: "When I am dealing with an angry teenager I don't look at the mouth or eyes now, I look at the brain, and it really helps!" There is no doubt that this knowledge has the capacity to alter relationships between young people and professional adults.

BUILDING A HEALTHY BRAIN

I will end this chapter with some thoughts about "healthy brains". To many, this is a new concept. Exploring this idea allows me to sum up the main messages of the book. I will first tell a story of a teacher who came to one of the very first workshops on the teenage brain run by my colleagues and me. This teacher was so enthused by what she had learnt that she went back to her school and developed an assembly all about the brain for pupils in Years 9 and 10. At the end of the assembly, she apparently said: "Off you go now, boys and girls, and beef up your prefrontal cortex".

I was delighted with this story. It meant that this teacher had seen that there is something we can all do to aid healthy brain development. It meant that she had seen that the brain is not a black box, but is something that is affected by the environment around us. We are not stuck with a particular brain. We can affect its development. The teenage years offer a special window of opportunity to influence how our brains develop.

In one of the focus groups I ran for teenagers, one young man actually said to me: "So, my brain is changing, and there's not much I can do about it". I was able to say: "No. There is a lot you can do about it!"

The teacher mentioned the prefrontal cortex. So why did she choose this site in the brain? As you will have read throughout this book, this site is sometimes known as the command and control centre of the brain. This is the site that manages thinking and reasoning, problem-solving and other intellectual activities. The more we can help this site become more mature, the greater the chance that we can act as rational beings. This will assist us in overcoming the influences of the amygdala and other areas of the brain that are to do with our emotions. We want all areas of our brains to change and mature, but the prefrontal cortex has a special role to play.

And then, what did this teacher mean when she used the phrase "to beef up your prefrontal cortex"? This leads us to a consideration of what a teenager can do to assist healthy brain development. I usually identify four things that can contribute to this process. These are:

- *Be curious.* By this I mean try and expand your interests and activities. Don't just do your homework, but extend your interests to other topics, take up a hobby, explore new things, stretch your brain!
- *Be proactive.* By this I mean use the internet in ways that are active rather than passive. If you are gaming, choose games that demand thinking and problem-solving. Don't be a passive observer, but be creative when you are on the screen.
- *Practice choice and decision-making.* In order to make decisions and choices, you have to engage your prefrontal cortex. So, try to find all possible ways that you can use this skill. The more you get involved in working out options and possibilities, the more your prefrontal cortex will be exercised.
- *Get more oxygen to your brain.* Oxygen is the food of the brain. The more we can get oxygen to our brains, the better they will function.

This means moving around, and not sitting still for long periods. The best way to contribute to a healthy brain is to be as active as possible.

This process applies to young people, but I should note that there are also things that key adults can do to contribute to this "beefing up". Here I would include having a greater understanding of brain development. This is hugely helpful for young people. Having talked this over with dozens and dozens of teenagers, I have learnt that having a parent or other adult who can be reassuring and knowledgeable about the brain makes a significant difference to a sense of well-being.

The next thing to note is that adults can do a lot to help with the ability to manage the variations in hormone balance. As we have seen throughout this book, one of the central elements of the developing brain is that, during this phase, the hormone balance goes up and down to a considerable degree. There are many strategies that can be developed to manage this volatility. Learning about relaxation, meditation, mindfulness and other practices that assist young people to manage wild swings of mood and emotion can be hugely helpful.

Finally, we should note the importance of routines. In Chapter 6, I mentioned the importance of good sleep routines in overcoming the melatonin effect. There is a big role here for parents in assisting young people to develop these routines in order to manage the impact of the hormonal balance. Of course, routines are not only appropriate for sleep, but are essential in other aspects of life, such as doing homework, getting to school on time, and so on. There is no doubt that one way to improve the functioning of the prefrontal cortex is to develop good routines. Such routines provide structure to everyday life, and this structure will require the involvement of the prefrontal cortex.

CONCLUSION

In this chapter, I have outlined why understanding the teenage brain is essential for all adults, but particularly for parents, carers and professionals who work with young people. I have mentioned the workshops that I and my colleagues have been running, and have given an example of one of the activities that helps us point the participants to the importance of understanding the teenage brain.

I have spent some time discussing the challenges inherent in the parenting of young people. I have outlined the STAGE framework and noted how it highlights five key elements of good parenting for this age group. I ended the chapter by talking about the healthy brain, and I showed how teenagers and adults can do something to assist with this process of enhancing good brain function.

The information contained in this book represents new knowledge. You may argue about whether this is really new. It is approximately 20 years since brain imaging became available as a tool to explore the human brain. Nonetheless, the information that we have gained as a result of this technology is only gradually becoming known to the general public. In addition, we are only at the very beginning of our understanding. Brain imaging only tells us so much.

We now know how much change is occurring during the teenage years, but there remains a long way to go on this exciting journey. Even during the course of writing this book, new information has been published. The next few years will tell us a lot more, and the technology of brain imaging will become even more sophisticated. It is my hope that you, the reader, will have enjoyed the book. Most importantly, though, I hope it makes your relationships with young people that much more rewarding.

FURTHER READING

Coleman, J (2019) "*Why won't my teenager talk to me? 2nd Edition*". Routledge. Abingdon, Oxon.

Coleman, J (2021) "*The teacher and the teenage brain*". Routledge. Abingdon, Oxon.

Downshire, J and Grew, N (2018) "*Teenagers translated*". Vermillion. London.

Jensen, F (2015) "*The teenage brain: a neuroscientist's survival guide to raising adolescents and young adults*". Harper. New York.

REFERENCES

CHAPTER 1

Jandial, R (2019) *"Life lessons from a brain surgeon: the new science and stories of the brain"*. Chapter 14. The younger brain. Penguin Life. London.

McRory, E, et al. (2017) Childhood maltreatment, latent vulnerability, and the shift to preventative psychiatry: the contribution of functional brain imaging. *Journal of Child Psychology and Psychiatry*. 58.338–357.

Rutter, M, et al. (1998) Developmental catch-up, and deficit, following adoption and severe global early privation. *Journal of Child Psychology and Psychiatry*. 39.465–476.

Thomas, M, et al. (Eds.) (2020) *"Educational Neuroscience: development across the life span"*. Chapter 2. An introduction to brain and cognitive development. Routledge. Abingdon, Oxon.

Ward, J (2015) *"The student's guide to cognitive neuroscience: 3rd Edition"*. Chapter 2. Introducing the brain. Psychology Press. London.

CHAPTER 2

Hagell, A (Ed.) (2012) *"Changing adolescence: social trends and mental health"*. The Policy Press. Bristol.

Luthar, S (Ed.) (2003) *"Resilience and vulnerability: adaptation in the context of childhood adversities"*. Cambridge University Press. Cambridge.

Masten, A (2014) *"Ordinary magic: resilience in development"*. The Guilford Press. London.

Seligman, M (2011) *"Flourish: a new understanding of happiness and well-being"*. Nicholas Brealey Publishing. London.

Thomson, R (2011) *"Unfolding lives: youth, gender and change"*. The Policy Press. Bristol.

CHAPTER 3

Coleman, L and Coleman, J (2002) The measurement of puberty: a review. *Journal of Adolescence*. 25.535–550.

Ernst, M, et al. (2005) Amygdala and nucleus accumbens in responses to receipt and omission of gains in adults and adolescents. *Neuroimage*. 25.1279–1291.

Farello, G, et al. (2019) Review of the literature on current changes in the timing of pubertal development. *Paediatric Endocrinology*. 7.337–350.

Galvan, A and McGlennen, K (2013) Enhanced striatal sensitivity to aversive reinforcement in adolescents versus adults. *Cognitive Neuroscience*. 25.284–296.

Galvan, A, et al. (2006) Earlier development of the nucleus accumbens relative to the orbitofrontal cortex might underlie risk-taking. *Journal of Neuroscience*. 26.6885–6892.

Hagell, A and Shah, R (2019) Health behaviours. In *"Key data on young people: 2019"*. Chapter 4. Association for Young people's Health. London. www.ayph.org.uk

Hagell, A, et al. (2012) Trends in adolescent substance abuse. In *"Changing adolescence: social trends and mental health"*. Chapter 7. Hagell, A (Ed.) Policy Press. Bristol.

Mendle, J, et al. (2019) Understanding puberty and its measurement: ideas for research in a new generation. *Journal of Research on Adolescence*. 29.1.82–95.

Romer, D (2003) *"Reducing adolescent risk: towards an integrated strategy"*. Sage Press. New York. Page 32.

CHAPTER 4

Bergman-Nutley, S and Klingberg, T (2014) Effect of working memory training on working memory, arithmetic and following instructions. *Psychological Research*. 78.6.869–877.

Blackwell, L et al. (2007) Implicit theories of intelligence predict achievement across adolescent transitions. *Child Development*. 78.246–263.

Gazzola, V et al. (2007) The mirror neuron system. *Neuroimage*. 35.

Mills, K A, et al. (2016) Structural brain development between childhood and adulthood. *Neuroimage.* 141.273–281.

Owen, A, et al. (2010) Putting brain training to the test. *Nature.* 465.775–778.

Thomas, M, Ansari, D and Knowland, V (2019) Educational neuroscience. progress and prospects. *Journal of Child Psychology and Psychiatry.* 60.4.479.

CHAPTER 5

Adolfs, R (2009) The social brain: neural basis of social knowledge. *Annual Review of Psychology.* 60.693–716.

Heaven, P (2001) *"The social psychology of adolescence".* Palgrave Press. Basingstoke, Hants.

Knoll, L, et al. (2015) Social influence on risk perception during adolescence. *Psychological Science.* 26.5.583–592.

Mills, K, et al. (2014) Is adolescence a sensitive period for social-cultural processing? *Annual Review of Psychology.* 65.187–207.

Nelson, E, Jarcho, J and Guyer, A (2016) Social re-orientation and brain development: an expanded updated review. *Developmental Cognitive Neuroscience.* 17.118–127.

CHAPTER 6

American Academy of Paediatrics (2014) School start times for adolescents. *Paediatrics.* 134.3.642–649.

Bonnar, D, et al. (2015) Evaluation of novel school-based interventions for adolescent sleep problems. *Sleep Health.* 1.66–74.

Bower, J and Moyer, A (2017) Effect of school start time on students' sleep duration, daytime sleepiness and attendance: a meta-analysis. *Sleep Health.* 3.423–431.

Cooper, R, et al. (2023) Development of morning-eveningness in adolescence: implications for brain development and psychopathology. *Journal of Child Psychology and Psychiatry.* 64.3.449–460.

Illingworth, G, et al. (2020) The teen sleep study: the effectiveness of school-based sleep education prorgamme. *Sleep Medicine.* December. 874–890.

Maskevich, S, et al. (2022) What time do you plan to sleep tonight? A longitudinal study of adolescent daily sleep regulation. *Journal of Child Psychology and Psychiatry.* 63.8.900–911.

Titova, O, et al. (2015) Sleep and academic performance at school. *Sleep Medicine.* 16.87–93.

CHAPTER 7

Baron-Cohen, S (2017) Neurodiversity: a revolutionary concept for autism and psychiatry. *Journal of Child Psychology and Psychiatry.* 58.744–748.

Hagell, A and Shah, R (2019) *"Key data on young people 2019".* The Association for Young People's Health. www.youngpeopleshealth.org.uk

Hollis, C, Livingstone, S and Sonuga-Barke, E (2020) Special issue: young people's mental health in the digital age. *Journal of Child Psychology and Psychiatry.* 61.837–940.

Immordino-Yang, M and Gotlieb, R (2020) Understanding emotional thought can transform educators' understanding of how students learn. In *"Educational neuroscience: development across the lifespan".* Thomas, M, Mareschal, D and Dumontheil, I (Eds.) Routledge. Pages 244–270.

Lavis, A and Winter, R (2020) Online harms or benefits? An ethnographic analysis of peer support around self-harm on social media. *Journal of Child Psychology and Psychiatry.* 61.842–854.

McRory, E, Gerin, M and Viding, E (2017) Childhood maltreatment, latent vulnerability, and the shift to preventative psychiatry: the contribution of functional brain imaging. *Journal of Child Psychology and Psychiatry.* 58.338–357.

Silberman, S (2015) *"Neurotribes: the legacy of autism and the future of neurodiversity".* Avery Publishing. London.

CHAPTER 8

Abela, A and Walker, J (Eds.) (2014) *"Contemporary issues in family studies: global perspectives on parenting support".* Wiley Blackwell. Chichester, West Sussex.

Gunnar, M (2023) Using parenting interventions as treatments and brain development. *Journal of Child Psychology and Psychiatry.* 64.3.345–348.

Howard-Jones, P (2011) From brain scan to lesson plan. *The Psychologist.* 210–213.

Lansford, J (2022) Annual research review: cross-cultural similarities and differences in parenting. *Journal of Child Psychology and Psychiatry.* 63.4.466–479.

Livingstone, S and Blum-Ross, A (2020) *"Parenting for a digital future".* Oxford University Press. Oxford.

Miller, A, et al. (2021) Deprivation and psychopathology in the Fragile Families Study: a 15-year longitudinal investigation. *Journal of Child Psychology and Psychiatry.* 62.4.382–391.